FINDINGS

VICKI HALPER

FINDINGS

The Jewelry of Ramona Solberg

BANK OF AMERICA GALLERY

IN ASSOCIATION WITH

THE UNIVERSITY OF WASHINGTON PRESS

Seattle and London

EXHIBITION SCHEDULE

Bank of America Gallery, Seattle, WA	November 8–December 14, 2001
Mint Museum of Craft + Design, Charlotte, NC	January 15–March 31, 2002
Museum of Craft & Folk Art, San Francisco, CA	April 16–June 15, 2002
National Ornamental Metal Museum, Memphis, TN	July 14–September 15, 2002

Copyright © 2001 by Bank of America

Printed in Hong Kong

Design by Michelle Dunn Marsh

The paper used in this publication meets the minimum requirements of American National Standard for Information Sciences—Permanence of Paper for Printed Library Materials, ANSI Z39.48-1984.

Sponsored by Bank of America

Library of Congress Cataloging-in-Publication Data

Halper, Vicki.

Findings : the jewelry of Ramona Solberg / Vicki Halper.

p. cm.

Catalog of a traveling exhibition held at the Bank of America Gallery, Seattle, Wash., Nov. 8–Dec. 14, 2001 and three other locations.

Includes bibliographical references.

ISBN 0-295-98157-1 (cloth : alk. paper) — ISBN 0-295-98158-X (pbk. : alk. paper)

1. Solberg, Ramona—Exhibitions. 2. Jewelry—Washington (State)—Seattle—History—20th century—Exhibitions. I. Title: Jewelry of Ramona Solberg. II. Solberg, Ramona. III. Bank of America (Seattle, Wash.). Gallery. IV. Title.

NK7398.S65 A4 2001

745.594'2'092—dc21

2001027689

CONTENTS

FOREWORD

While the art of the Pacific Northwest has frequently been associated with visionary painters such as Morris Graves and Mark Tobey, the region has also produced exceptionally important artists in the field of crafts. Working in this milieu is an artist who has been important, influential, and respected among her peers and within her field, but whose work has never been comprehensively exhibited. That artist is the jeweler Ramona Solberg, whose work is known for its invention, beauty, and humor. We at Bank of America are proud to support and participate in a national celebration of her masterful and thoroughly original oeuvre.

This exhibition and accompanying publication are produced on the occasion of Solberg's eightieth birthday. They are intended to document not only a lifetime of creative excellence, but also to recognize her generous spirit and rich legacy, carried forth by a new generation of artists in the field of fine art jewelry. More than seventy beautiful objects created by Solberg and others who have flourished within her sphere tell a story of quiet dedication, a perfect eye, and a love of the unusual and unexpected. The exhibition, set to travel to several cities throughout the United States, will bring Solberg's work before new audiences, and affirm her reputation as a living treasure here at home.

I would like to extend my heartfelt thanks to curator and author Vicki Halper for so expertly assembling the exceptional artworks that best illustrate Solberg's creative journey. Thanks go also to the collectors and institutions who have generously agreed to part temporarily with their beloved artworks so that they might be enjoyed and appreciated by others, and to the receiving museums who will present Solberg's work in cities across the country. Others who have labored tirelessly to ensure the success of the project include Jennifer Mills, Assistant Director, Bank of America Art Programs; photographer Rod Slemmons; Torie Stratton; the Northwest Designer Craftsmen Living Treasures Video Archive; Pat Soden and the staff at the University of Washington Press; and colleagues who spoke at length with the author about Solberg: Marjorie and Russell Day, Eveleth Green, Laurie Hall, LaMar Harrington, Lloyd Herman, Ron Ho, Mary Lee Hu, Hazel Koenig, Larry Metcalf, Kiff Slemmons, and Nancy Worden.

And finally, best birthday wishes and warmest thanks to the inimitable Ramona Solberg, for sharing her gifts and providing such leadership to the world of contemporary jewelry. She is indeed a living treasure, and we are all enriched by her offerings.

—PEGGY WEISS
Director, Bank of America Art Programs, Northwest Region

INTRODUCTION

The Wizard of Seattle

During a visit to Seattle on a Sunday afternoon in the fall of 2000, I asked Ramona Solberg whether the bracelet she was wearing was made by Charles Loloma. It was not a Loloma, she said, but a Ramona. Actually, she preferred to think of it as a Mondrian, and then told me this story.

In 1964, after a three-month, round-the-world trip, she took up residence at the University of Arizona as part of a sabbatical from her teaching position at Central Washington State College. In Tucson she frequented Tom Bahti's shop to admire his Southwest Indian collection. It was there she saw a Charles Loloma bracelet made of turquoise with a bit of coral. Unfortunately, it did not fit her wrist. The image of the bracelet stayed in her mind for two decades, until after retiring in 1984 she was invited to Tucson to conduct workshops for the department of Parks and Recreation. There, she decided to take advantage of the department's lapidary equipment and make herself a Loloma-inspired bracelet. Her Arizona hostess supplied her with a broken ivory bangle from India, some turquoise hishi beads, and fragments of ironwood: found objects, Ramona-style. There was not enough ivory to create the object she desired, but in the backyard she noticed a beef bone that had been chewed by the resident dog. Inspired by this find, she combined the bone, turquoise beads, and ironwood with a discarded piano key

and added branches of coral to fill in the gaps—and the Ramona bracelet emerged. She continues to wear it today, one of only three bracelets that she has ever made.

■ ■ ■

You enter a country kitchen which embraces you with its warmth, only to realize that the masonry jars you assumed were filled with jams and jellies are in fact stocked with buttons, shells, coral, and other treasures. What would have been the dinette is a studio space. In the midst of the adjoining room is a rich collection of textiles and artifacts indicating that the occupant has traveled around the globe. Ramona pulls open one of the cupboard drawers to reveal an orderly array of dominos. Another houses a hoard of amber beads—each one holds an accumulation of objects waiting for Ramona.

The chest of drawers in Lenore Tawney's New York studio loft comes to mind, a work of art begun in 1974 and known as a "collage chest." The drawers contain shells, découpage hands, the skull of a bird, feathers, tools—each drawer holding a mystery of life. With Ramona, in contrast, each drawer stores an encounter with a foreign native, an adventure in an exotic bazaar or marketplace, or a simple stroll in her adopted city of Seattle.

■ ■ ■

Ramona Solberg was born in 1921, three years after Kurt Schwitters's declaration that any "material or object could be combined for the purposes of equal evaluation, and that restrictions to a single material are one-sided and narrow-minded." [1] This dictum informs all her work, beginning in the late 1960s when she embraced a diversity of multicultural objects and assembled them into new forms and meanings.

Non-precious fragments become precious in the private universe she creates. Her iconography consists of unexpected and often idiosyncratic juxtapositions—glass beads from Africa, shells, milagros from Mexico, dominos, dice, and found objects from antique stores and from friends. Her innovative combinations lift the fragments out of their primary, primordial origins and into a global sphere. When she includes a commercially molded metal toy or car, these fusions take on a narrative character as the diverse elements become as expressive as paint and canvas. Like a shaman's necklace or a talisman, Ramona's works embody and protect the wearer, while documenting her own thoughts and travels.

Ruth Penington, Ramona's teacher at the University of Washington, stressed elements of design, color, and composition, moving her toward a "free form amoebic shape." In the 1950s, Ramona's work reflected western artistic trends. An early brooch responds to the modernist spirit, not unlike Manhattan's Irena Brynner, Paul Lobel, Ed Weiner, and the San Francisco artists Peter Macchiarini, Margaret de Patta, and Bob Winston.

Influenced by other cultures and by fellow artists such as Don Tomkins, who came to Ellensburg, Washington, in 1965, her personal aesthetics soon emerged, and she became a pioneer in the assemblage of found objects.

Ramona may have been frequently "on the road," but she did not stop at her peers' studios, attend conferences and workshops, or join organizations such as the Society of North American Goldsmiths (SNAG). Instead, she traveled, taught, and exhibited in exotic places, such as Afghanistan, India, Mexico, Scandinavia, South America, Europe, and China. When asked whether she had a dialogue with her colleagues in other parts of the country, Ramona exclaimed, "I used to look at them in *Craft Horizons* and say 'Wow!' I was so intimidated that I never applied to SNAG. [My work] was always different."

However, she did become involved with the American Craft Council following the rise of regional crafts organizations and guilds in the late 1940s and early 1950s. As secretary of the World Crafts Council, she attended conferences in Dublin in 1970 and Istanbul in 1972. She became acquainted with fellow craftspeople working in other media, such as Don Reitz, Sam Maloof, Paul Soldner, Mary Nyburg, and Rose Slivka, the former editor of *Craft Horizons*. Perhaps it was her passion for travel and people that led her to this involvement when she normally shied away from national organizations and conferences.

In 1969, Ramona's work was selected for inclusion in *Objects: USA*, the first major survey of American crafts. This inaugural exhibition, held at the National Collection of Fine Arts of the Smithsonian Institution, [2] proclaimed a new era for these artists, whose medium was not part of the mainstream. Her presence in this exhibition and in *Good as Gold* (1982) brought Ramona greater national and international attention. She holds a unique place in the history of contemporary jewelry, dismissing traditional techniques such as casting and not participating in most national or international exhibitions. Her energy went into her regional community and her work, and the individuals who surround her are not unlike an extended family. The influence she has exerted on other Seattle artists, including Laurie Hall, Kiff Slemmons, Ron Ho, and Nancy Worden, is extraordinary. Their works freely incorporate rulers, pencils, bones, and coins. Each of these artists maintains a distinct personal identity, while the peripatetic Wizard of Seattle is central to their lives and ideas.

· · ·

There is a range of expression and diversity of temperament among other artists who shared with Ramona the use of discarded objects and assemblage. Sam Kramer defied tradition and "titillated" the public with the use of teeth and taxidermist eyes as central motifs in his surrealist jewelry. J. Fred Woell rejected precious materials. He created modern-day icons using images from comic strips, refuse from bullets, punctured beer-can lids, and Coca-Cola tops. The late Japanese-born Miye Matsukata often used historical found objects such as Roman coins, Egyptian fragments, pre-Columbian artifacts, and Noguchi-like pebbles, all elegantly combined with constructed silver and gold. Known for his works executed in cloisonné, William Harper would incorporate rattlesnake rattlers, carapaces of beetles, and bones, which when assembled, became ornaments reminiscent of primitive fetish objects. Judy Onofrio's brooches are assembled from fragments of costume jewelry, beads, shells, tin cans, and hand-carved elements, making grand brooches which could be mistaken for 1940s jewelry.

In Europe, among those working with found objects were Falko Marx and Bernhard Schobinger. Marx transformed the rusted top of a sardine can into a brooch set with precious stones from a bracelet; he immersed a nineteenth-century porcelain medallion in water, afloat with gold, silver, rubies, and diamonds. Schobinger has made jewelry out of broken tops smoothed and strung on a cord, and a drain plug became the shank of a ring set with diamonds or carborundum. Pierre Cavalan from Australia assembles shells, bottle tops, watch findings, and souvenir tacks making complex necklaces, commemorative medals which cite occasions of historical importance. As with these artists, anything and everything becomes an important element for Ramona: objects which have outlived their usefulness, become obsolete, or been cut off from their original context are preserved and given a new life.

· · ·

The image of Ramona standing above her work table with a blowtorch, soldering a piece as if she were tending to a barbecue, conveys her distinctive presence. Her spirit of adventure and her passion for people have allowed her to record, through her works, an important aspect of the taste of our time. Can you imagine an archaeologist in the future discovering a piano key next to a carved beef bone set with turquoise and coral? Each element holds a secret—the origins of the bone, the walrus tooth, the dominos, the stash of coral and beads—all held together by a remarkable person with a singular vision in the history of twentieth-century jewelry. As Ramona has stated in her video biography, "they will never figure out how these cultures got together." [3]

—HELEN W. DRUTT ENGLISH

——————————— NOTES ———————————

1. John Elderfield, *Kurt Schwitters* (London: Thames and Hudson, 1985), p. 49.
2. The National Collection of Fine Arts, Smithsonian Institution, was renamed the National Museum of American Art in 1985, and renamed the Smithsonian American Art Museum in 2000.
3. *Ramona Solberg—Jeweler, Teacher, Traveler*, directed by Ann Coppel, produced by the Living Treasures Committee of Northwest Designer Craftsmen, Seattle, 2000.

Findings

VICKI HALPER

Findings

The briefest synopsis of Ramona Solberg's life so far might read: Born in South Dakota; visited India fifteen times; enjoys life; makes necklaces.

Solberg's Norwegian pioneer roots are the foil for the repeated pull of cultures more various, more vibrant, more colorful, and more ancient than her own. She has approached these cultures, as she has approached all aspects of her life, with a positive, expansive disposition. "Why do it if it's not fun?" has been her motto for most of her eighty years.[1] Solberg's necklaces, composed with small objects often collected on her travels, reflect her curiosity and delight, as well as a compelling desire for an order that is both rigorous and beautiful—a modernist ideal derived from both Bauhaus and Scandinavian design. Her jewelry's straightforward construction and imposing scale reflect her own direct manner and substantial build. "Don't insult a large person with a too delicate piece," she has counseled.[2] "Ramona was never one to do trinky-dinky little jewelry," her sister Eveleth Green has remarked.

Solberg's urges to travel and to create art were initiated by the mixture of admiration and envy that a kid sister has for much older siblings. Eveleth was twelve years old when Ramona was born. By the time Solberg was in elementary school in Seattle, Eveleth was in college. "She was popular, she was pretty, and she wore awfully cute clothes; she was an art major and she was always doing interesting things. I wanted to grow up and be just like her," Solberg recalls. In a University of Washington jewelry class taught by Helen Rhodes, Eveleth made a ring with a Rhodenite stone that led Solberg to vow that she herself would one day make a similar piece. "I wasn't an outstanding artist; I just plodded along," Solberg says of her early years, attributing any successes to a "teacher so old she remembered my sister."

Arley, Solberg's brother, was thirteen years her senior and a fisheries major in college. He spent summers working on the President Line, which sailed to the Orient, and spent a year sailing around the world after he quit college. Travel was good for him, according to Solberg. "He used to be finicky, but pretty soon he could pick a cockroach out of his soup. . . . He sent home these wonderful letters and pictures and I thought what could I possibly do? I wish I were a boy." Arley returned home with photos, stories, and exotic objects purchased with the money he saved as a non-drinking, non-poker-playing seaman: swords from the Philippines, pajamas from China, kimonos and wooden clogs from Japan. To Ramona, travel meant stories of interesting places and people and wonderful objects that were not just mementos of places visited but compelling embodiments of other cultures.

One-year-old Ramona with her siblings Arley and Eveleth, South Dakota, 1922

Sergeant Solberg in Heidelberg, Germany, ca. 1946

Before World War II, Solberg's travels were limited to family visits to her midwestern relatives: "Minnesota and back; Minnesota and back." She enlisted in the army in 1943 as a patriotic college senior who "really didn't know anything" and was a poor typist, choosing the Women's Army Corps (WAC) over the navy because of the possibility of working overseas. Stationed at Fort Ogelthorpe, Georgia, for basic training, she braved the heat dressed in unbecoming khaki ("I looked like a calsamined wall"), and enjoyed her first taste of what she considered "girl's camp," an experience she had missed as a child because of strapped family finances during the Great Depression. "I enjoyed every

minute, even KP," is her characteristic assessment of a situation many have found less appealing.

Solberg was stationed in Tulsa as a recruiter for aviation cadets and WACs. "I made PFC running a mimeo machine," she says of her achievements there. Later she worked at Brook General Hospital, San Antonio, in Troop Information and Education, helping "TBs, VDs, worms, and psychos" get their high school diplomas. In Texas she voted for the first time, throwing off her father's conservative, dictatorial yoke when casting her absentee ballot for FDR. In her words, "I waved good-bye to Dad."

In 1945 Solberg reenlisted, jumping at the chance to go overseas, and spent the next three years as an Information and Education sergeant in Germany, abroad at last. She was spared combat and the experience of seeing the German concentration camps, which had been emptied before she arrived. The army confirmed her ease with leadership and her comfort with foreign places. "Going into the army was the best thing I could have done," Solberg says of that time of her life. "It gave me a feeling of confidence. I felt that I could do practically anything. . . . I could go anyplace in the world and never feel that I was in danger." Solberg was also unaware of sex discrimination during these years: "I never suffered by being a woman. No one ever said, 'Ramona go and make us some coffee.' I was a sergeant; they had to behave themselves."

Art wasn't much on Solberg's mind then. Her college education as an art major was on hold, and although she visited museums wherever she went, she made no art. Her career plans were vague. As a youngster she had dreamed of becoming a nurse, airline stewardess, or fireman. The army experience led her to consider journalism and sociology. Architecture, a subject to which she was attracted, was sadly out of the question—she was poor in math. She eventually decided to get her teaching certificate because she already had a few credits in education and, with summers free, "I thought maybe I could travel."

And travel she did. When Solberg returned from the army in 1950, just one course short of her bachelor's degree and out of sync with the academic year, she took advantage of the GI Bill and went to Mexico with her mother to study weaving and jewelry-making at Bellas Artes in San Miguel de Allende and at Universidad de Michoacan in Morelia. She briefly considered marriage while there, but decided against a union that would necessitate her becoming a

Ruth Penington. Untitled necklace (cat. 66)

Catholic ("Why should *I* be the one to convert?") and living far from her Seattle home. "We almost got married; finally I left," she remarked offhandedly. Nieces, nephews, and students would become the children in her life.

Solberg describes the jewelry she made in Mexico as little different from the pieces she had been making with Ruth Penington, her formidable professor at the University of Washington. Penington, an early modernist jeweler who worked in silver, was "serious and formal," according to art historian LaMar Harrington, while Solberg, who was "fun and meandering," appeared to be one of the few students who aroused her interest. Solberg credits Penington with instigating her career as a jeweler by giving her an A, Ramona's first in art. However, the confidence and boldness one associates with Solberg's jewelry were not a result of her studies with Penington, whose exacting manner and style restrained Solberg's natural exuberance. And while Penington made a lasting impression on Solberg with her use of beach pebbles and her incorporation of a pre-Columbian figure in a ring, Penington almost never incorporated man-made objects, as opposed to natural materials, in her work, a hallmark of Solberg's mature style.

In Mexico, when Solberg fabricated a silver pendant with hints of traditional Scandinavian design and placed a pre-Columbian ceramic earplug at its center (pl. 1), she was moving away from Penington's and her own previous work by incorporating cultural artifacts and by mixing cultures with a nonchalance that presaged her later work. She also made a bib-like necklace etched with Mexican designs (p.7), moving closer to the bold forms that would become her trademark. Upon returning to Seattle, however, Solberg continued in a more traditional manner, combining pearls or dentalium shells with silver, for example, in comparatively delicate compositions.

In 1951 Solberg began teaching at James Monroe Junior High School in Seattle. She thought she had chosen teaching in order to have summers to travel, but she fell in love with the work and with her students. She had been asked to take a coveted position in Seattle even before she got her certificate, but she postponed entering the profession for one year in order to complete her degree. "I really liked it. I *had* to have a job, but I *loved* it. The kids were so funny!" With four nephews of junior high school age, Solberg knew the territory well, and she had an easy way with authority, developed during her years as a sergeant. She admits without guilt that she "didn't run the tightest ship in the world."

During her first two years as a schoolteacher, Solberg took night classes at Edison Vocational School in Seattle, in order to use the jewelry facilities there. Coralyn Pence, who taught the class, brought in "bits and pieces" from the South Pacific gathered by her sea captain father.

These souvenirs reinforced Solberg's association of jewelry-making with wanderlust.

In 1953 Solberg took a one-year leave of absence from teaching, again using the G I Bill, to study jewelry-making, particularly enameling techniques, in Norway. She was accompanied by a nephew and her mother, with whom she had lived ever since her father died during the last days of her army service. As a widow, Betsy Solberg ("a neat, funny lady") had been asked by each of her children to live with them. Ramona considered herself lucky to have her mother's company and attention for the remainder of Mrs. Solberg's life.

The enameling techniques that Solberg learned in Norway enabled her to incorporate more color into her jewelry, and her work abroad became the impulse for her 1957 Master of Fine Arts thesis, written during her early years as a teacher. She decided to pursue a graduate degree when her friend, jeweler Russell Day, suggested she join him in the endeavor, remarking that she would command a higher salary with an M.F.A. degree. Solberg chose her topic, "Variations in Decorative Materials as Combined with Metal in Jewelry," because of a "love of color."[3] In her thesis, Solberg states the importance to her of the Celtic and Viking jewelry she had seen in Scandinavia, particularly at the Oslo Etnografisk Museet where she spent many hours sketching Iron Age pieces.

Among the techniques Solberg utilized in her thesis pieces were champlevé enameling (glass powders placed in shallow pockets cut out of the metal base), *basse-taille* (glass powders placed on a sculpted surface leading to variations in enamel translucency), incrusted enamel (opaque colors painted directly onto a roughened surface), and gilding (covering) with gold foil. She incorporated beads, shells, bone, and pearls into some of these pieces, often suspending

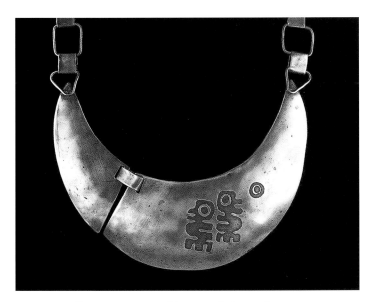

Ramona Solberg. Copper necklace made in Mexico, 1950

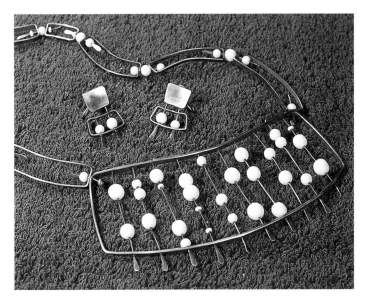

Ramona Solberg. *Abacus*, 1957, silver and glass beads

them from silver frames on wires pounded flat at the ends to hold them in place, as in *Abacus*, a piece now lost. Rivets became important visual elements—"making mechanics of the jewelry part of the design," she wrote in sympathy with modernist aesthetics. Two pieces used pebbles gathered at the end of her year abroad: "I became so involved with this honesty of material that I made the pendant and pin . . . of unpolished beach pebbles picked up on an impoverished vacation in Spain." She concluded, "I am now anxious to go further into the realm of unusual combinations as long as the end result is an honest treatment of the material and not just spectacular sensationalism."

Solberg's thesis work allied her with those jewelers who, like her teacher Ruth Penington, were in the geometric rather than the surrealist camps of modern art. Their work tended towards cool abstraction, with neither the biomorphic shapes nor oblique narrative references of jewelers like Sam Kramer in the surrealist camp. By the 1940s many jewelers were using simple and direct construction

techniques like Solberg's rivets and forged (pounded) wires, usually under the influence of Alexander Calder, the great American sculptor whose jewelry had been frequently exhibited with his sculptures as early as 1929. The New York jeweler Ed Weiner, enchanted with Calder's wire sculptures and shifting mobiles, made his *Abacus* brooch in 1950, threading beads onto wires strung in a silver frame, as Solberg did in several of her thesis pieces. Weiner noted that the abacus "incorporated a theory of gravity-generated motion not too distantly related, in my mind, to the mobile. My interest was to mount colored and semi-precious stones in a new way." [4]

Pebbles regularly appeared in mid-twentieth-century jewelry, as in Betty Cooke's brooch from about 1950, in which a flat ribbon of silver bisects a smooth, black stone, placed on its edge, or Margaret De Patta's brooch from later in the decade, in which three pebbles, a pearl, and a band of silver form a rigorous abstract composition. Kramer used cowry shells and glass taxidermy eyes in his

Solberg during videotaping of "Gadget Printing," Ellensburg, Washington, ca. 1956

pieces before 1950. Enameling, which Solberg more or less abandoned after her thesis, and ebony and ivory, materials Solberg would use much later with consistency and great effect, had been adopted by Earl Pardon in the early 1950s.[5] Solberg knew of these jewelers from black-and-white reproductions in the magazine *Craft Horizons,* and, while she was not a pioneer in the use of these materials, she clearly threw in her lot with the modernists and their clean designs, straightforward techniques, and use of non-precious materials.

Shortly before completing her M.F.A. thesis, Solberg took a teaching position at Central Washington State College in Ellensburg (now Central Washington University), a two-hours' drive east from Seattle across the Cascade Mountains. Like her junior high school position and her later professorship at the University of Washington, the Central job was a fluke, never sought; her greatest ambition had been to teach high school. She says, looking

back, "I'm always at the right place at the right time. I always feel it's pure, dumb luck." The secretary of the University of Washington Art Department had called her in without warning for an interview with the president of Central. She was offered the job ("I was so flattered!"), and in 1956 she moved to Ellensburg with her mother in time for fall classes.

At Central, Ramona taught in two departments: Industrial Arts and Art—metals, leather, printmaking, art history, five preparations a week, just like junior high school. "I was queen of the two-hour class," Solberg remarked of the ease of her transition to college teaching. Among Solberg's new friends in Ellensburg were her colleague Ed Haines, an art historian, and his wife Juanita Haines, a jeweler. Their extensive collection of ethnic jewelry gave Solberg her first prolonged exposure to the indigenous arts of Africa, the Indian subcontinent, and Latin America. The boldness, color, and improvisational qualities of this jewelry would have a lasting effect on Solberg and, in turn, on the many other jewelers in the Northwest who would encounter similar pieces through exhibitions Solberg later curated in Bellingham, Bellevue, and Seattle.

Solberg also met Seattle professor Gloria Huntington in Ellensburg, where Huntington was researching Indian beaded bags. Huntington asked Solberg to make her a necklace using rolled coppers and trade beads, and she paid for the work in beads. Huntington also introduced Solberg to her neighbor in Seattle, Ron Ho, an artist and schoolteacher who would become a close friend and colleague.

In the mid-1960s, when Solberg wanted another jeweler to join her in the department, she wrote to Don Tompkins (1933–1982) at Syracuse University, where he was teaching while getting his master's degree. She had first met Tompkins about 1950 when he was a precocious

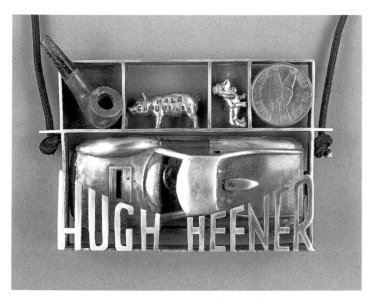

Don Tompkins. *Hugh Hefner*, ca. 1970 (cat. 71)

eighteen-year-old working as a gofer for Russell Day at Everett Community College. Day recalls that Tompkins, who was not then enrolled as a student and had never made jewelry, had begun creating wonderful pieces at home using a flat iron and blow torch on plebeian materials— beer bottle caps, spoons, and broken glass. Tompkins later studied with Ruth Penington and received his bachelor's degree at the University of Washington.

Tompkins arrived in Ellensburg in the fall of 1966 with his East Coast wife, Betty (who hated living in the boonies), his knowledge of Pop Art, and his 1960s disregard for authority, including the aesthetic kind. He had spent the previous summer working for a Philadelphia jeweler, Wesley Emmons, who gave him free rein when he proved unsuitable as an assistant and repairman. Rummaging through a hoard of cheaply cast metal charms, Tompkins conceived the Commemorative Series of pendants, the first few of which became production items for Emmons's business.[6] The basic format for the series was a subdivided

rectangular grid in which each compartment held a found object. In *Hugh Hefner*, for example, a later one-of-a-kind pendant, Tompkins subdivides a large rectangle into smaller ones that each hold a found object or a casting. The pendant is hung from a simple, knotted cord. This treatment, which combines the grid associated with abstract art with the found and populist materials associated with assemblage and pop art, is a treatment that Solberg also began to elaborate upon, then permanently adopted, sometime after Tompkins became her teaching colleague.

"He really loosened me up!" Solberg remarked of Tompkins. "I was tight after Ruth." She seemed immune to Tompkins's satirical bent and political agendas, but benefited from his fearless use of man- and machine-made objects of little intrinsic value, and from the sense of humor, sometimes wicked, that infiltrated his work. Both shared an impeccable sense of composition and a love of cheap cultural artifacts, and both used the subdivided rectangle as a pendant format.[7]

A rectangular framing device is behind Solberg's abacus-like construction, and she had employed the subdivided rectangle by the late 1950s, in a pendant consisting of joined segments of ebony, brass, silver, and bone (cat. 6). But Solberg made a significant leap when she began to treat the rectangle as a frame for found objects in about 1967, when she first incorporated dominos, the found object with which she is most readily identified, into a pendant (pl. 4). She attached three dominos, two face forward, one face backward, to a silver base using exposed rivets, and hung the pendant from a forged silver band, a treatment she rarely used in later work, preferring a simple leather or rubber cord.

Solberg found the dominos at a Seattle thrift store, where they must have immediately drawn her attention

1. Pendant with earplug, 1950
Silver, pre-Columbian clay earplug (cat. 1)

because they were small, cheap, made of ebony and bone (materials she would always favor), boldly black and white, and starkly geometric. She paid no attention to the domino as a game piece and made no reference to players or winnings. Solberg, who finds gambling distasteful, is, however, a proponent of having fun and considers herself a very lucky person. The very benignity in her use of gaming pieces may reflect her charmed relationship with life's chances; she has no ax to grind with Lady Luck.

The domino necklace was sold in 1968 at the second World Crafts Council in Lima, Peru, where Solberg exhibited her work. (The first Council had been held in Los Angeles.) Another piece she exhibited there, *Shaman's Necklace* (pl. 5), was chosen by Lee Nordness and Paul Smith for the groundbreaking exhibition *Objects: USA*, whose catalogue was a virtual listing of the major figures in the American crafts world for decades to come. The piece, with its beautiful whiteness and mix-and-match cultural artifacts, verges on narrative, but its mystery is that of a casual mix of strange, ordinary, and beautiful objects chosen for their color and form more than for their content. Solberg wrote in the catalogue: "Long a collector of curios, I found some of my 'treasures' too small for satisfactory display. I assembled favorite objects into jewelry, and recalling the magic necklaces of the Northwest Indians, called this piece *Shaman's Necklace*." [8] In Solberg's hands, the necklace becomes a portable treasury or *Schatzkammer*, the German term for Renaissance collections of man-made and natural marvels that were housed in special rooms.

Central was a wonderful place to teach during Solberg's years there. Tompkins and Solberg formed such a dynamic department, one that was so relaxed and congenial, according to their colleague William Dunning, that you "couldn't beat the students off with a stick." After work

"Flopsy and Mopsy." Solberg (left) with colleague Hazel Koenig, Seattle, 1977

Solberg returned to a house she had designed and built. Nevertheless, Solberg left Ellensburg in 1967 when Spencer Moseley, the new director of the University of Washington School of Art (1967–1977), asked her to teach during Ruth Penington's sabbatical leave. When Solberg said she could not "leave my secure position for the unknown," Moseley offered her a permanent position as a tenured faculty member, which she accepted. Solberg taught in the School of Art's Metal Design and Art Education programs until 1983, when long-simmering dismay with departmental politics prompted her slightly early retirement.

When Solberg arrived at the University of Washington in 1967, the importance of art education, the applied arts (e.g., interior design), and crafts were unquestioned. Moseley, a fine abstract painter in the synthetic cubist tradition, had been one of three writers of a how-to book for teachers (*Crafts Design: An Illustrated Guide*) and would later write an article about Solberg's jewelry for a national crafts publication.

One of his co-authors on *Crafts Design* was Pauline John-son, head of art education, who, with Penington, head of metals, and Hope Foote, head of interior design, formed a coterie of strong women professors within the umbrella of the art department. When Solberg and colleague Hazel Koenig joined the School of Art in 1967, however, they were the first women to be hired in thirteen years. Solberg became particularly close with Koenig, who was her office mate and neighbor for sixteen years. They shared an assem-blage aesthetic, a love of travel, and a belief in art education for the masses, and they worked together on films and exhi-bitions. Their friend and colleague Larry Metcalf reports that his mother called them Flopsy and Mopsy because "they looked like such fun!"

On Christmas Eve 1972, Solberg's mother, wearing a red dress and waiting for her daiquiri, died suddenly at the age of eighty-six. Solberg was in Mexico, researching an educational film about Latin American folk art with Koenig and Jack Stoops, a former professor of art education from UCLA. "I didn't go into deep mourning, as that was some-thing Mother would not have wanted," Solberg remarked, citing only a great burst of activity as a change in her own behavior—"I didn't mope; I worked." In short order, she completed the thirty-minute film, created four more educa-tional film strips, produced a book on jewelry-making, and expanded her travel schedule.

Solberg's travels outside Europe and North America had begun in 1964, when she took a nine-month sabbatical from Central. She bought an around-the-world airplane ticket (ten stops for $999) and, starting in Tokyo, traveled alone to Thailand, Cambodia, Vietnam, India, Lebanon, Jor-dan, Egypt, Turkey, and Greece. She spent the remainder of the sabbatical studying at the University of Arizona. (Her second sabbatical, from the University of Washington in 1975, was cleverly divided into three successive winter terms, each spent roaming the Eastern Hemisphere.) Shortly before her mother's death in 1972, Solberg attended the World Crafts Council meeting in Istanbul (she had been secretary of the United States Committee of the Coun-cil since 1970). After the meeting she joined Jack Lenor Larsen and Sam Maloof, two of the most honored figures in the American crafts world, in a trip to the Middle East.

After Solberg's return from Istanbul, Penington, then president of Seattle's Friends of the Crafts, one of the city's first support groups for local artisans, asked her to lead a tour for the organization; the destination would be her choice. So in 1973 Solberg returned to Turkey, Afghanistan, and Iran with twenty-three people in tow. It was a great trip "except for the closure of the Beirut airport," she recalled, casually brushing off the unexpected cancellation of their sojourn in Lebanon. This trip initiated Solberg's fifteen-year career as tour guide, usually under the auspices of a local travel agency or the University of Washington Contin-uing Education Department, and often with many of the same old friends in her groups.

Solberg also returned to Europe, spending three sum-mers teaching with Jack Stoops in England (1973, 1974, and 1976). The two organized and led "Design Resources of London" for groups of students and art instructors taking the ten-credit course, which was sponsored by the Univer-sity of Washington. In London markets, as in markets worldwide, Solberg collected beads and odd bits and pieces, "curios," as she called them—objects that would fit in her pocket, would cost little, weigh little, and eventually find their way into her jewelry or into her drawers and drawers of materials waiting to become jewelry. The caliper in *Button Rule* (pl. 14), for example, was bought at London's Bermondsy Market.

Not surprisingly, Solberg had little time for jewelry-making during these years, although she created necklaces for exhibitions when asked. (When pressed for time and ideas, she'd grab a domino, particularly if she was showing at a gallery for the first time.) In addition to teaching and touring, she also published a how-to book for teachers, which led to a great demand throughout the country for her presence as a workshop leader.

Inventive Jewelry-Making (1972) was written in one summer, with Solberg enlisting her students, former students and *their* students, and colleagues (including Rudy Kovacevich, Ron Ho, and Laurie Hall) to fabricate new works to illustrate the book. Other illustrations used existing pieces and examples of ethnic jewelry from the collections of her friends. In the flood of do-it-yourself crafts publications printed at that time (like the lower-end Lothrop Craft Books series which included *Sock Craft, Kitchen Carton Crafts*, and *Jewelry from Junk*), her book stands out through its intelligence and wit and the extremely high quality of its examples.

The jewelry to be created with the aid of the book would be of the "inexpensive and expendable variety," Solberg wrote, and the techniques would be simple and direct—"sawing metal and wood, melting plastic, and bleaching bone." Sewing, gluing, and tying would be used in place of soldering. The objective was "imaginative pleasure."

Among her own pieces illustrated in the book are a felt necklace with inset mirrors echoing Indian textiles (cat. 15); a necklace squeezed from tubes of Doodley-Doo, a heat-set plastic packaged for children (pl. 9); and a "peace pendant" with a ban-the-bomb symbol, an eagle, and the text of a Nixon speech about the bombing of Cambodia— the only political piece ever created by the artist (cat. 12).

Found objects are everywhere in the book, and a chapter is dedicated to their use. Solberg defines the found object as "anything manufactured for another purpose, and then put to use by the craftsman or artist." She notes the relationship of found-object jewelry to assemblage, Dada, and Pop Art, and she states: "Jewelry of this kind is often extremely sophisticated, and this approach is perhaps the most contemporary mode of any of the jewelry-making techniques considered in this book." In a warning reflecting her own strict design ethic, however, Solberg tells her readers to beware of "visual bedlam." She controls the field in her own illustrated pieces by using a leather-covered anchovy can to frame a collection of metal and plastic objects, and by clearly separating wool, string, feathers, and beads into separate pouches for an "amulet" formed by stitching through two vinyl rectangles. (The amulet is lost. Similar construction is shown in pl. 8.)

Inventive Jewelry-Making is an engaging and delightful book, suggesting the non-hierarchical, fun-loving, straightforward, and curious woman behind it. It is probably not a publication that would help an art professor achieve tenure today, and in that sense it symbolizes the spirited populism that would be lost when the School of Art began to divide the educators from the artists. After Spencer Moseley resigned as director in 1977, departmental politics became increasingly strained. Reorganization undercut the independence and equality of the various branches of the arts: Fine Arts faculty freely denigrated the Art Education Department; the Interior Design Department was closed, and Art Education was under constant threat of the same. (Art Education was finally abolished shortly after Solberg left.)

In 1983 Solberg retired, two years short of her expected date. In 1985 she returned to the house she loved in Ellensburg and stayed there until 1989, when she moved back to Seattle ("that's where the action is"), having grown tired of driving over the Cascade mountains day after day while curating the *Ubiquitous Bead* exhibition for the Bellevue Art Museum. Retirement meant that Solberg had more time to make jewelry, and her production consistently increased through the 1990s, when she was creating some of the best pieces of her career.

Before Solberg left the University of Washington, she had been working in the three general modes that continue to distinguish her necklaces—formalist, mimetic, and thematic.[10] Her formalist mode encompasses those pieces in which found objects are chosen and arranged primarily for their abstract qualities—for example, most of the necklaces incorporating game pieces. The jeweler Kiff Slemmons reports Solberg saying at the end of the 1990s: "Of course I love circles. Circles and squares are what it boils down to for me." The jeweler Nancy Worden paraphrases Solberg's approach as: "I just grab whatever looks good and throw it in there." But this is throwing like a great baseball pitcher.

It is Solberg's marvelous ability to know what "looks good" that creates such rigorous harmony between a white-tipped fur hat ornament, a spotted Indian ivory bead, and a half-moon piece of Alaskan walrus tusk in *Bavarian Brush* (pl. 30), a recent necklace in which subtlety and power are matched. This way of working is fundamental to Solberg and occurs throughout her career with undiminished strength. It starts with a few seed objects pulled out of treasure-stuffed drawers. These are arranged on paper while Solberg inks the outlines of the silver frame and clasp. This scale drawing of the final piece, with found objects in their proper place, is discarded when the necklace is completed.

Solberg's mimetic mode includes the many necklaces in which the artist fabricates silver elements to echo the design or structure of found parts such as millefiori beads (pl. 7), ivory chain (pl. 6), and coral beads (pl. 17). Such

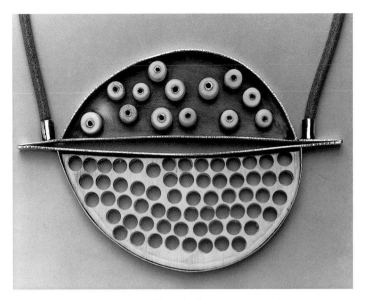

Ramona Solberg. Ivory necklace before reconstruction, 1985 (see pl. 27)

echoing is a primary way that Solberg incorporates her beloved beads into necklaces and honors them by the added value of her attentive craftsmanship. The greatest concentration of the mimetic pieces is in the 1970s, although they are not limited to that time.

Thematic pieces include those necklaces in which found objects are associated by subject matter. *Cracker Jack Choo Choo* (pl. 23), for example, combines a map fragment, a compass, and a silver cast of a plastic train found in a candy box. The thematic pieces tend to be concentrated in Solberg's later career, and their creation has probably been nourished by her community of jeweler-friends, including Laurie Hall and Kiff Slemmons, who work thematically or conceptually. Unlike those jewelers, Solberg rejects interpretative analysis of her pieces. She would say that the *Choo Choo* piece is not a paean to travel but is instead the random result of finding a nice plastic train. As for *Watership Down* (pl. 12), she says the pendant reflects a confluence between a student's gift of a rabbit charm (which Solberg then cast in silver, modifying the ears in some castings), and her then-recent reading of the novel of the same name. She was amused that a major character in the novel was the rabbit Hazel, and says she had no idea that she and her own friend Hazel Koenig were known as Flopsy and Mopsy, siblings of the rabbit Peter Cottontail in the child's story. If there are other hidden stories, Solberg won't say. "Ramona is open in the sense of generous, and open with opinions, but otherwise is closed," a good friend noted.

Solberg's thematic necklaces are more the result of free association than deep deliberation. For her, consideration of meaning is secondary to consideration of design. Often very little separates a formalist piece from a thematic one. In 1985, for example, she made a brilliant formalist pendant using a discarded piece of ivory from which Indian beads had been cut (p.13). In that necklace she translated the stark black/white, positive/negative spaces of her domino pieces into an imposing oval format. When the piece was dropped in the late 1990s, shattering the ivory, Solberg riveted it back together and used a cast silver bee to hide some of the breaks. The ivory, you see, reminded her of a honeycomb, and the necklace, which would originally have been purely formalist, became thematic (pl. 27). When Solberg integrates a small hand into a formalist game-piece pendant, as in *Look I'm a Winner* (pl. 31), she adds a thematic twist to an arresting abstract composition, and then seconds it by the title.

A Community of Jewelers

The younger jewelers with whom Solberg has been associated—Ron Ho, Laurie Hall, Kiff Slemmons, and Nancy Worden—are generally united in their use of silver, interest in cultural artifacts, focus on necklaces of substantial scale

Ron Ho. *The Kingfisher and the Tigers*, 1990 (cat. 65)

among the possible jewelry formats, and commitment to pieces that are comfortably wearable. It is in their insatiable search for content in their creations that they most differ from their senior colleague.

In 1966 Solberg traveled from Ellensburg to Seattle to lead a summer workshop at Bellevue Community College in which schoolteacher Ron Ho participated. Ho, then a painter, says he had always been interested in studying jewelry but was "terrified of Ruth Penington," a common reaction. Solberg was, on the other hand, "warm and wonderful." In the 1966 workshop Solberg handed out dominos from the cache she discovered at Seattle's Goodwill thrift shop, the same cache she had used to create her own first domino necklace (pl. 4). The piece Ho made and gave to Solberg was stolen in 1969; he re-created it for

Laurie Hall. *An Account*, 1994 (cat. 63)

Lloyd Herman's 1981 exhibition, *Good as Gold*, which highlighted modern jewelry in non-precious materials.

Solberg freely takes credit for Ho's "becoming Chinese" in his jewelry. "Ron," she remembers telling him, "you drink too much Coca-Cola." Wherever the credit may belong, she encouraged him to embrace his Asian background, and it is true that when Ho began to concentrate on found objects from the Orient, and later to fabricate pieces depicting objects such as Chinese chairs, his work became more distinctive. A Ho necklace is structurally more complex than a Solberg; it often has greater fluidity, and it is hung with forged metal, as was Solberg's first domino piece, rather than cord. Like Solberg, however, he continues to frame found objects in silver, the strong compositional device that also pays homage to the

findings, and to place necklace catches at the front or side for the wearer's ease.

Laurie Hall, then a teacher at Mercer Island High School just east of Seattle, first met Solberg when the latter juried her work into a late-1960s Bellevue arts and crafts fair. Hall attended a teacher's workshop given by Solberg in the fall of 1969 and, impressed with the affinity between Solberg's jewelry and Pop Art, realized "finally, I know what I can do." Hall also took Solberg's class the following summer, and the teacher's praise of her work there ("We have one person here who is a designer!") was so exciting that Hall "could hardly stand it."

Hall considers Solberg a master of the "get-your-shit-together-you-can-do-better-than-that" look, and says she was "a woman who seemed bigger than Mom." But jewelry was only one facet of what made Solberg impressive. She was about "life, adventure, color, design, recombining what you see, and stories that you tell." Hall was hugely affected by the ethnic jewelry that Solberg showed, but eventually she realized that she herself could only use objects from her own history and its pioneer American roots. For many years Hall has rarely used found objects at all but has fabricated miniatures of things she has seen. "I'm going to make my own found objects," Hall decided early on. "You find them with your eyes, and then you make them."

An Account is Hall's response to a huge and remarkable installation by the artist Ann Hamilton at the Henry Art Gallery in 1992. Hamilton had covered the floor with tarnished and numbered metal locker tabs, had blackened the walls with flames and wax from burning candles, and had set live yellow canaries loose in the room. In the necklace, Hall captures her own feelings about restriction and freedom in that space. "Locker" becomes "lock her"—an armored collar that, according to Hall, is "a play on how necklaces lock you in." The numbered tags, fabricated by Hall along with the lock pendant, represent hoards of people and hoards of money "all locked up." She credits Solberg as the source of her ability to conceive that such tags could be jewelry (see, for example, Solberg's use of numbered tags in *Series 2*, 1972, pl. 11), and that this jewelry could express a roomful of content.

"I knew Ramona's work before I knew Ramona, so she was no surprise," Kiff Slemmons says of her first meeting with Solberg at a jewelry symposium at the Oregon School of Arts and Crafts in Portland in the early 1970s. Slemmons, whose extensive academic background is in language and literature rather than in fine arts, found the jewelry community too technically oriented and "snotty," except for Solberg. She uses the term "vitality" to describe Solberg's work and person: "Ramona was interested in the vitality of objects," and "I still see her as a beacon of vitality, of connection with the world."

Before meeting her, Slemmons had gone "a million times" to the 1970 ethnic jewelry exhibition Solberg curated for the Whatcom Museum of History and Art in Bellingham, Washington. The show, which included pieces from the collections of Gertrude Husk and Solberg, had "a tremendous impact" on Slemmons. She became attentive to Solberg's own work from that time on. The two artists were attracted to similar things, and Slemmons credits Solberg with directly inspiring her in "the spirit of using non-precious materials" and "the framing of objects." Slemmons, however, became dissatisfied with simply choosing beads and objects to highlight: "I was making shrines to these objects. They were doing all the work. I wanted more that came from me." In 1985 she realized she would either have to stop making jewelry or commit to it wholly as an artist, not an artisan. That same year she instigated an exhibition called *Lost and Found*

at the Traver-Sutton Gallery in Seattle which helped codify the link between Solberg, Hall, Ho, and herself. Slemmons suggested that each of the artists create a piece of jewelry for the exhibition using an object to be chosen by Solberg. She believed that the differences between the jewelers would be clarified if each worked with the same raw materials.[11]

Solberg characteristically chose dominos and created *Chicago Fire* (pl. 18) as her own contribution. This necklace is vintage Solberg: The three ivory dominos placed side-by-side have various combinations of one and two black dots, with the twos always following the same diagonal and the ones exhibiting the eccentric placements often found in handmade objects. They make a pattern that is austere and lively at the same time, the jeweler's unmatchable trademark. Three buttons are symmetrically arranged over the dominos—a four-hole ivory button on either side of a silver one announcing the Chicago Fire Department—and form an architectural pediment to the game pieces. The ivory buttons are white circles, while the domino dots are black. The buttons' holes are negative circles, while the domino dots are positive. The silver button, largest circle of all, celebrates good, honest labor, a theme that Slemmons strongly identifies with Solberg (see, for example, the overall buttons in *Pay Day*, cat. 11, and the measuring tool in *Button Rule*, pl. 14). But this is not a necklace about firemen or human toil. Rather it is a nuanced abstraction that gently humanizes the grid.

Ho's pendant, *Full Fathom 5*, is hung from silver instead of the cord that Solberg used. His three dominos are asymmetrically stepped and are topped with two disks and a jaunty Chinese fish (perhaps Ho's earliest use of an Asian object); each found object is framed independently. As usual, his piece is the most reminiscent of a Solberg.

Hall's necklace, *Dominant Factor*, is the only one without a pendant. Dominos, dice, and a bone hand set in

Kiff Slemmons. *Hands of the Heroes: Ramona*, 1991 (cat. 69)

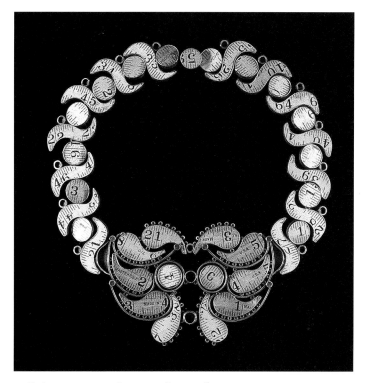

Kiff Slemmons. *Paisley*, 1998 (cat. 70)

silver are strung to form a squared-off U. The artist stated that she had trouble making this piece, since found objects are not the source of her inspiration. Rather she searches for or re-creates artifacts to follow her ideas.

Slemmons seems to have been free-associating— ivory domino, tickling the ivories, piano player, Fats Domino! In her pendant, a small black hand sits atop two horizontal dominos and is reaching for a set of miniature piano keys made of silver. *Fats Domino* is first and foremost thematic, a forerunner to the Hands of the Heroes series that cemented her reputation. In that series, a simple template of a hand is used as the basis for brooches honoring those whom the artist deems worthy. The pin honoring Solberg, for example, gives the jeweler a life-line of beads.

In *Paisley*, a recent necklace, Slemmons cuts a straightedge ruler into the baroque forms of Indian paisley. The piece hints at all sorts of dichotomies—straight versus curved patterns, linear versus non-linear thinking, European versus Asian culture, analysis versus decoration, a Westerner appropriating Indian dress. Slemmons's use of the ruler would never be confused with Solberg's, although the senior artist brought both measuring sticks and India into the sight lines of Northwest jewelers. "Ramona thinks of me as an intellectual," Slemmons remarks. "She thinks I take it all much too seriously."

Nancy Worden did not participate in the Traver-Sutton exhibition, but she is considered one of the crew by Solberg and has been a strong link between Ellensburg and Seattle jewelers.[12] In the early 1970s, Worden's high school

Nancy Worden. *Viper's Venom*, 1998 (cat. 74)

teacher in Ellensburg was Kay Crimp, a former student of Solberg's, and Worden learned of Solberg's work through slides as well as by seeing originals around the necks of art community locals. One necklace in particular, with stone beads and hollow, cagelike, cast metal beads, became "permanently imprinted on my brain," Worden recalls. By the time Worden met Solberg at the Ellensburg community art gallery run by Solberg's sister, Eveleth Green, the artist had reached "mythological proportions" in her mind. In about 1976 the art gallery also showed Solberg's collection of ethnic jewelry. Worden recalls, "I'd never seen anything like that before." She was deeply attracted by the variety, playfulness, and heavy ornamentation in the collection, in contrast to what was usually valued in her formal education: "When I was in school, everyone was going for the sleek."

Solberg had by then left Ellensburg. In 1972 Worden, a high school senior, became a protégée of jeweler Ken Cory, who had replaced Don Tompkins at Central. She studied with Cory for six full years, and she was introduced to found object jewelry by him, not by Solberg. Like most jewelers a generation or two younger than Solberg, Cory searched found objects for meaning rather than visual delight, and he taught his students to do the same. This attitude, as well as a heightened sensitivity to cultural appropriation, has discouraged the incorporation and dismantling of found objects from distant cultures. All the artists in Solberg's coterie are more likely to use found objects from their own cultures, American or Asian, because that is where meaning resides for them and because they fear misusing or misrepresenting a foreign artifact. Solberg herself has generally had no hesitation in using found objects, or parts of found objects, in her necklaces. She sawed an African ivory bracelet into sections for *Kimono* (pl. 28), for example, while Slemmons, who possesses a similar bracelet, cannot cut into hers.

Worden moved to Seattle in 1981, after graduate study at the University of Georgia, Athens, and became a friend of Solberg's later in the decade. In the mid-1990s Solberg asked her to make something for an exhibition she was curating, the 1996 *Ubiquitous Bead II*, follow-up to a popular 1987 Bellevue Art Museum extravaganza also organized by Solberg. For that exhibition Worden made her first beads since her student days with Ken Cory (*Initiation Necklace*, cat. 73, for example). The necklace she made for the Bellevue exhibition, formed of beads made from IBM Selectric typewriter balls, was the cover illustration for *Ornament* magazine in Autumn 1996 and is her best-known piece. "I've been making beads ever since that necklace."

Viper's Venom is a necklace about alcoholism and is intentionally "evil and ominous," Worden states. Saddened by a friendship that ended because of drink, Worden, the most technically oriented of the jewelers discussed here, made beads out of beer bottle caps (chosen for their color), champagne corks (chosen for shape), coins (ready-made metal disks from the estate of Ken Cory, who died prematurely in 1994), and cobra skin. Worden notes that the drinker becomes "a viper," and that the snake has long been associated with "tempter and devil." The central bead is a cork fishing float covered with taxidermy eyeballs ("spooks") and studded with nails, a detail inspired by a nail-studded Congolese *nkondi* figure in the Seattle Art Museum. "Definitely my Ramona piece," Worden says of this tour-de-force in beads.

Worden calls Solberg "my best critic." She recounts a discussion they had while Worden was struggling over a very complicated necklace:

Solberg: "What is *that*!? Why do you have that stuff on the back?"
Worden: "It's essential to the idea."
Solberg: "Get rid of it!"
Worden (in essence): "Yes, ma'am."

When Solberg looks at the jewelry created by her friends, her first question is "Does it look good?" not "What does it mean?" This artist, who has fostered a community of strong-minded artists bewitched by content, would herself go for the gut—harmony, strength, wearability, delight. If Solberg were guarding the Pearly Gates, she'd be asking jewelers, "Were your designs good?" and "Did you enjoy your life?" No one would be the worse for following her example and answering yes.

NOTES

1. All quotations are from interviews with the author conducted between September 1999 and November 2000, unless otherwise stated.

2. *Inventive Jewelry-Making* (New York: Van Nostrand Reinhold, 1972).

3. University of Washington, March 22, 1957.

4. Quoted in Toni Greenbaum, *Messengers of Modernism: American Studio Jewelry, 1940–1960*, (Paris and New York: Flammarion and Montreal Museum of Decorative Arts, 1996), p. 32. *Abacus* is illustrated in fig. 79.

5. Ibid. Fig. 18 (De Patta); figs. 29, 30, 31 (Kramer); fig. 64 (Cooke); figs. 82–84 (Pardon).

6. Conversation with Betty Tompkins, Oct. 4, 2000.

7. Tompkins almost certainly knew the work of J. Fred Woell, the American jeweler who was a pioneer in the use of found objects, or, more accurately, cultural discards, to make political statements. Woell would have no direct influence on Solberg, and his self-denigration and sometimes bitter debunking were not her style. Solberg robustly embraced life without anguish or anomie; Woell, on the other hand, wrote: "Life is a joke—a bad joke. My work is like that—a bad joke . . . . Man is a disaster. We can't save ourselves." Quoted in Donald J. Willcox, *Body Jewelry, International Perspectives* (Chicago: Henry Regnery, 1973).

8. Lee Nordness, *Objects: USA* (New York: Viking, 1970), p. 205.

9. Spencer Moseley, Pauline Johnson, and Hazel Koenig, *Crafts Design, An Illustrated Guide* (Belmont, California: Wadsworth, 1962; Spencer Moseley, "The Necklaces of Ramona Solberg," *Craft Horizons*, June 1973.

10. Solberg herself divides her jewelry into the categories "sweet, dug up, and found," or pieces focused on beads, natural materials (bone, coral, ebony), and man-made objects.

11. The four necklaces are reproduced in *Ornament*, Autumn 1986, p. 17.

12. For descriptions of jewelry traditions in Ellensburg see Ben Mitchell, *The Jewelry of Ken Cory: Play Disguised* (Tacoma, Washington: Tacoma Art Museum, 1997), and Matthew Kangas, "Ellensburg Funky," *Metalsmith*, Fall 1995.

1. Pendant with earplug, 1950
Silver, pre-Columbian clay earplug (cat. 1)

2. *Mitla*
(pendant/brooch),
ca. 1951 Silver,
pre-Columbian clay
artifact (cat. 2)

3. **Pendant with
pebbles, ca. 1957**
Silver, gold leaf,
beach pebbles,
leather (cat. 5)

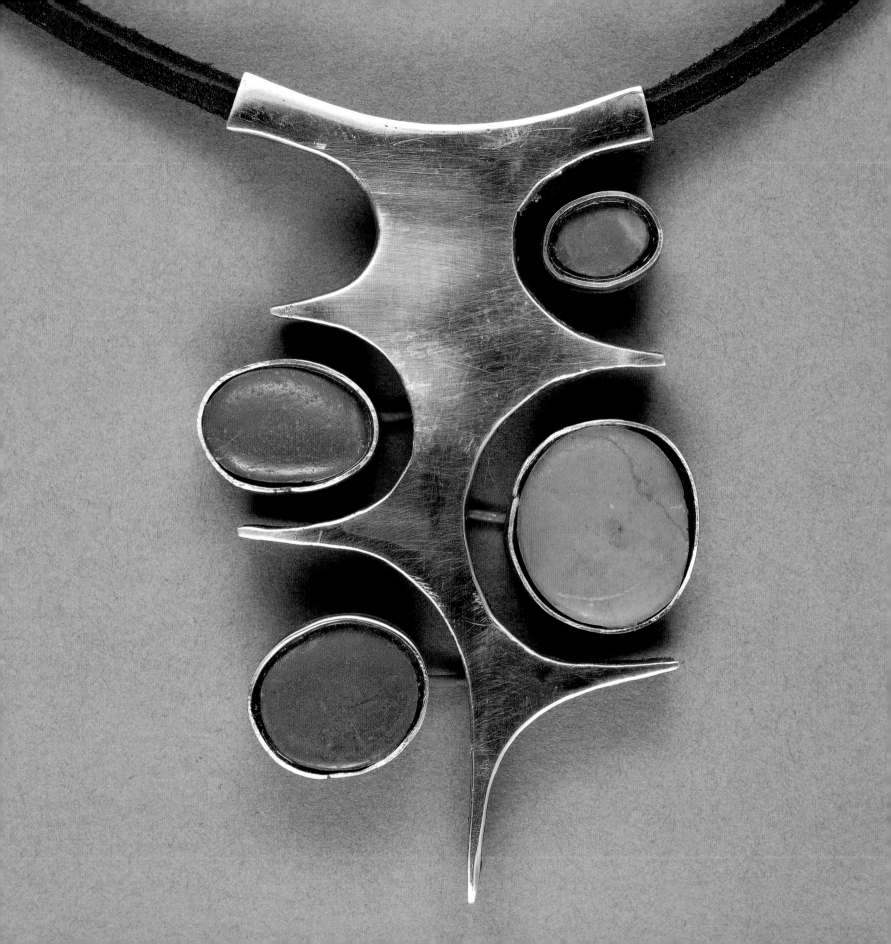

24

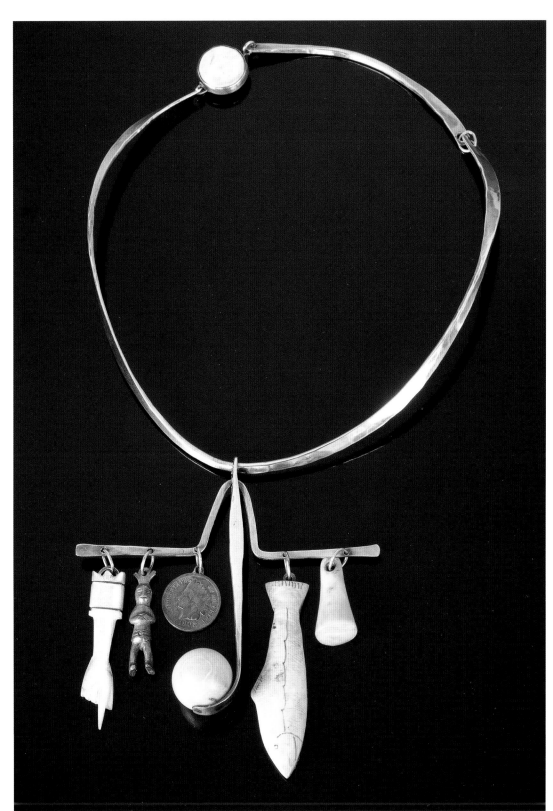

4. Domino necklace, 1967 Silver and dominos (cat. 9)

5. *Shaman's Necklace*, 1968 Silver, penny, Brazilian *figa*, Guatemalan *milagro*, Alaskan artifacts (cat. 10)

25

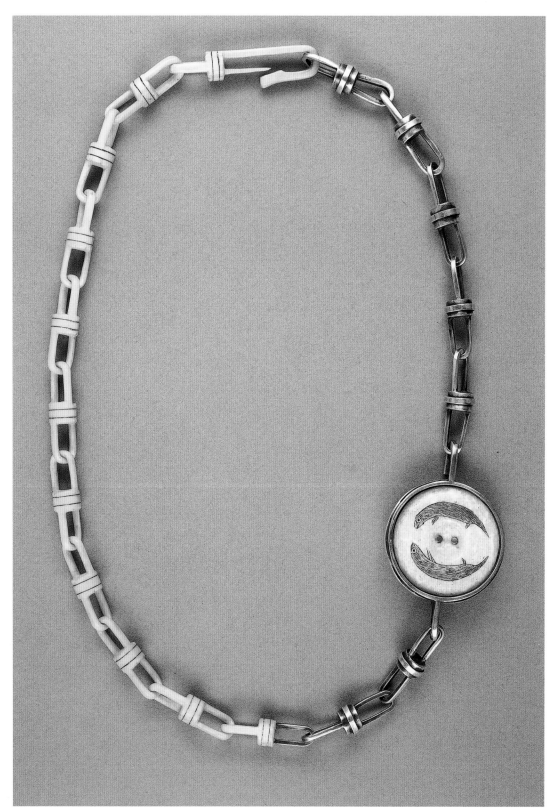

6. *Eskimo Chain*, ca. 1970 Silver and Alaskan ivory artifacts (cat. 13)

7. **Millefiore necklace, ca. 1972** Cast silver and African millefiore beads (cat. 17)

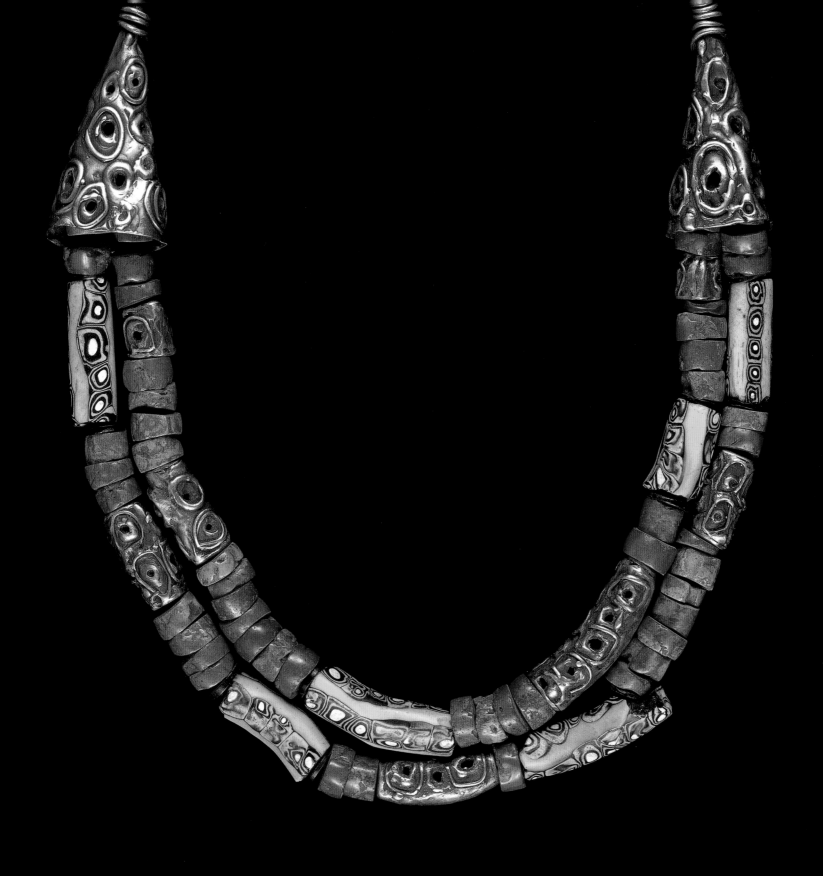

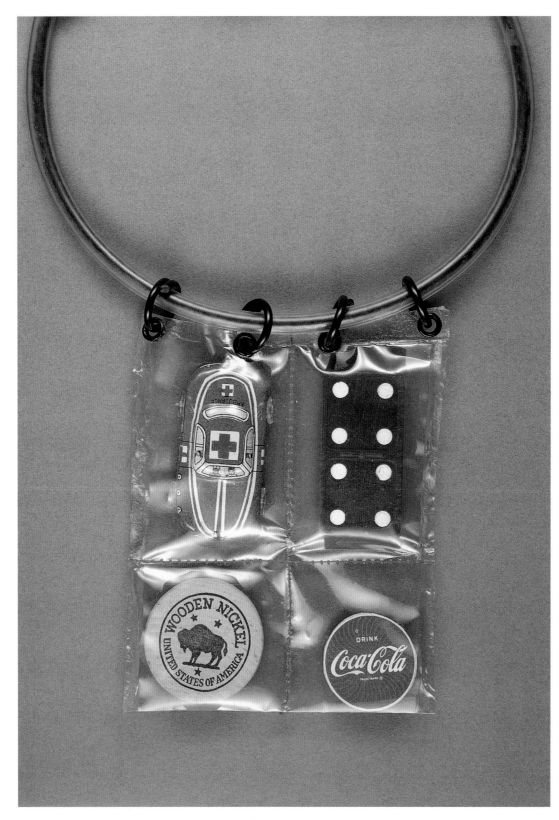

28

8. Plastic pouch necklace, 1972
Plastic, chicken leg bands, found objects, yarn (cat. 16)

9. Doodley-Doo necklace, 1972
Doodley-Doo (PVC) (cat. 14)

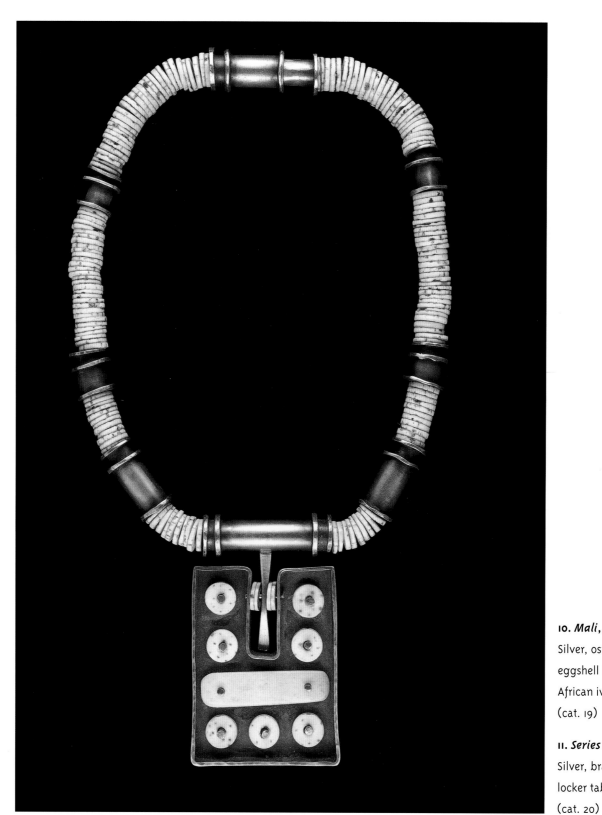

10. *Mali*, **1972**
Silver, ostrich
eggshell beads,
African ivory
(cat. 19)

11. *Series 2*, **1972**
Silver, brass ship and
locker tabs, leather
(cat. 20)

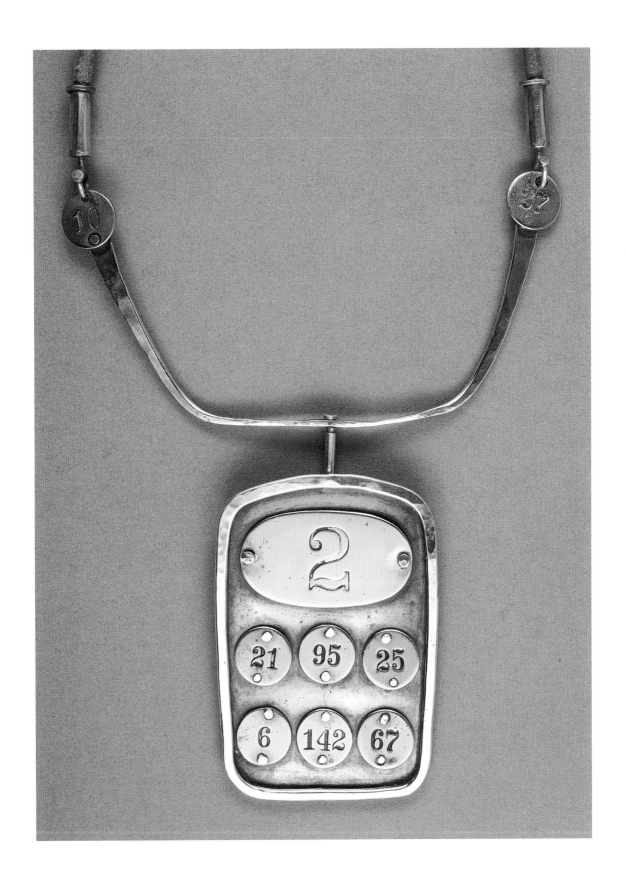

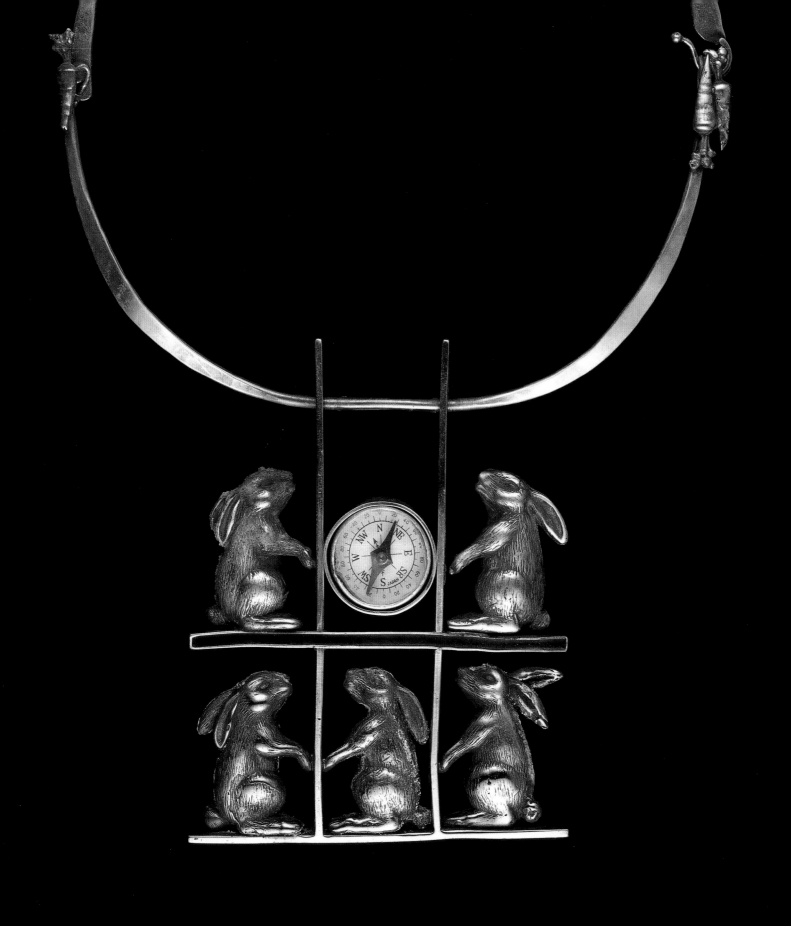

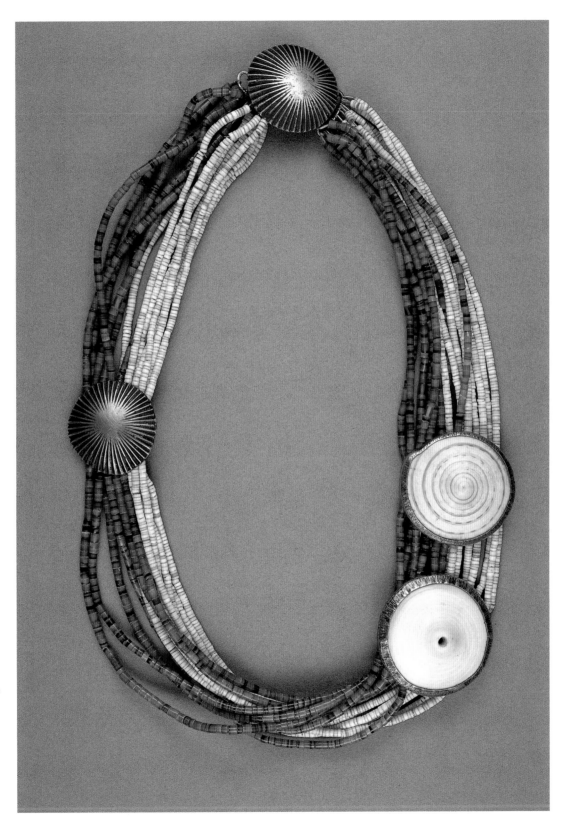

12. *Watership Down,*
1978 Cast silver and
compass (cat. 27)

13. *South Pacific,*
1979 Silver and
shell beads (cat. 28)

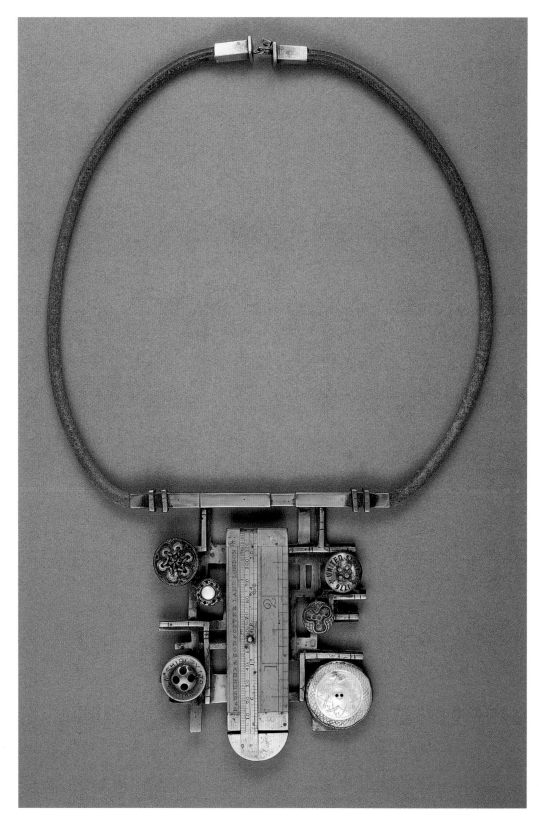

34

14. *Button Rule,* 1981
Silver, found buttons
and caliper, leather
(cat. 29)

15. *Ampersand,* 1982
Silver, found ivory
ampersand, ruler,
leather (cat. 31)

36

16. African bottle bead necklace, 1983

Cast silver and glass beads (cat. 34)

17. Coral necklace, early 1980s

Electroformed silver and coral beads (cat. 36)

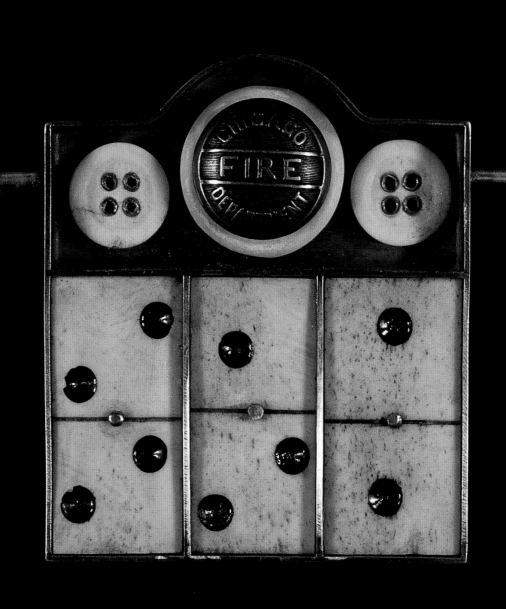

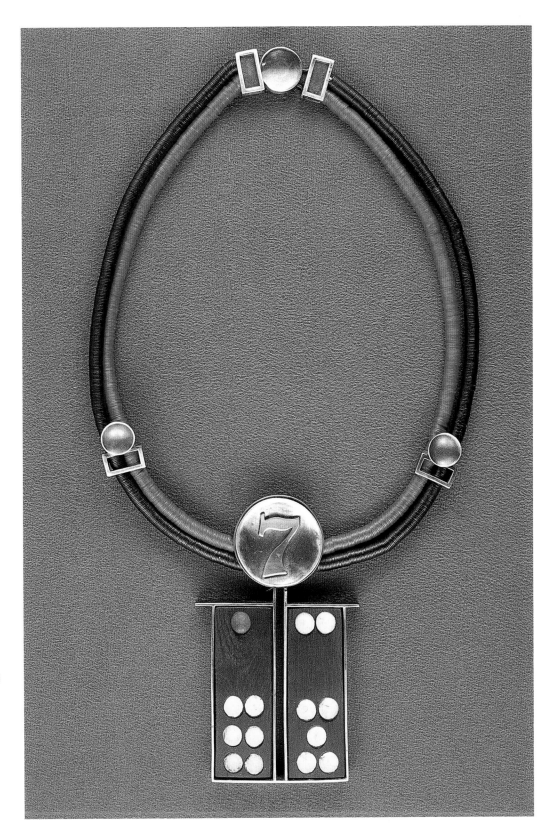

18. *Chicago Fire*, **1985**
Silver, dominos, buttons, leather (cat. 37)

19. *Lucky 7*, **1986**
Silver, Czech plastic disks, ebony game pieces (cat. 38)

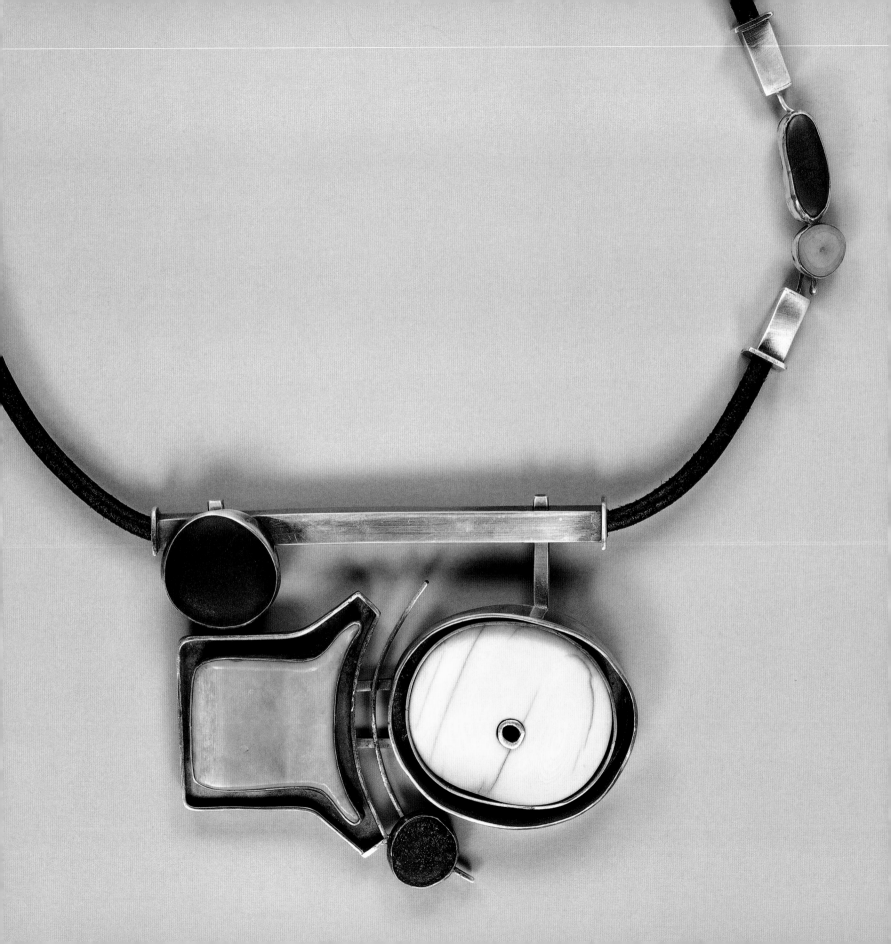

20. *Labrets*, 1991
Silver, pebbles, African
and Eskimo labrets,
leather (cat. 46)

21. *Lucky 13*, ca. 1992
Silver, domino, dice,
cord (cat. 47)

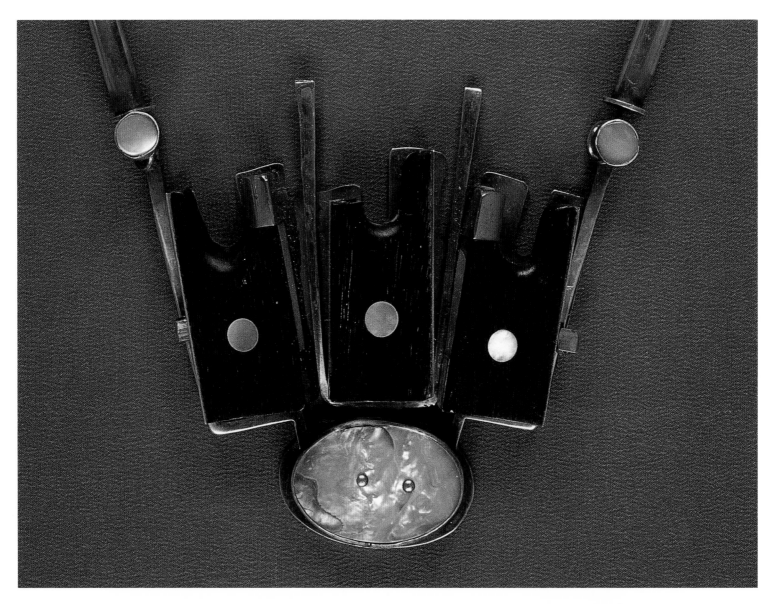

22. *Bow Regards*, 1994
Silver, violin bow parts, Victorian
mother-of-pearl pin, rubber cord (cat. 49)

23. *Cracker Jack Choo Choo*, 1995
Cast and forged silver, compass, map,
button, Lucite, leather (cat. 52)

43

24. *Time Flies*, **1995** Silver, clock
face, bone ornament, plastic
fly, rubber cord (cat. 53)

25. *Indian Bank*, **1995** Silver,
copper, coins, tin bank, leather
cord, electroformed arm.
Arm electroformed by
Nancy Worden (cat. 54)

46

26. *Mr. McGregor's*, **1996,** Silver, Chinese ivory rabbit, enameled carrot, millefiore beads (cat. 55)

27. Necklace with bee, 1985, reconfigured in 1997 Cast silver, Indian ivory, Lucite, bone beads, leather (cat. 56)

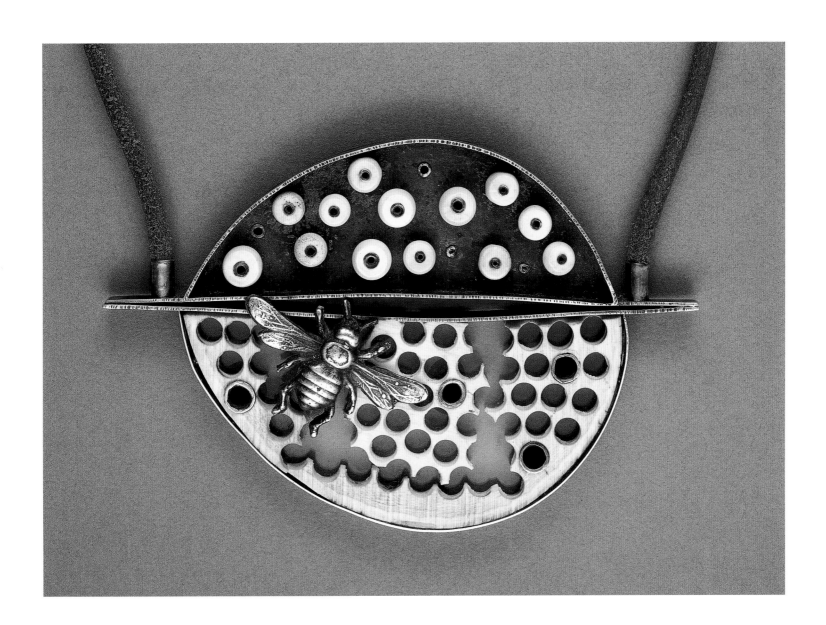

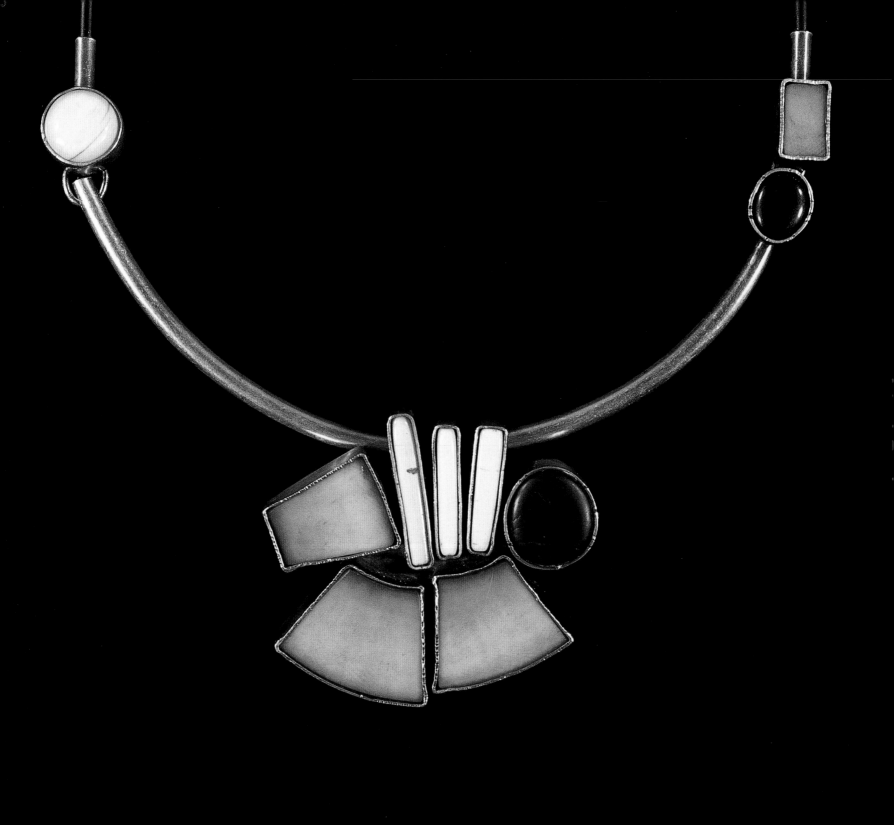

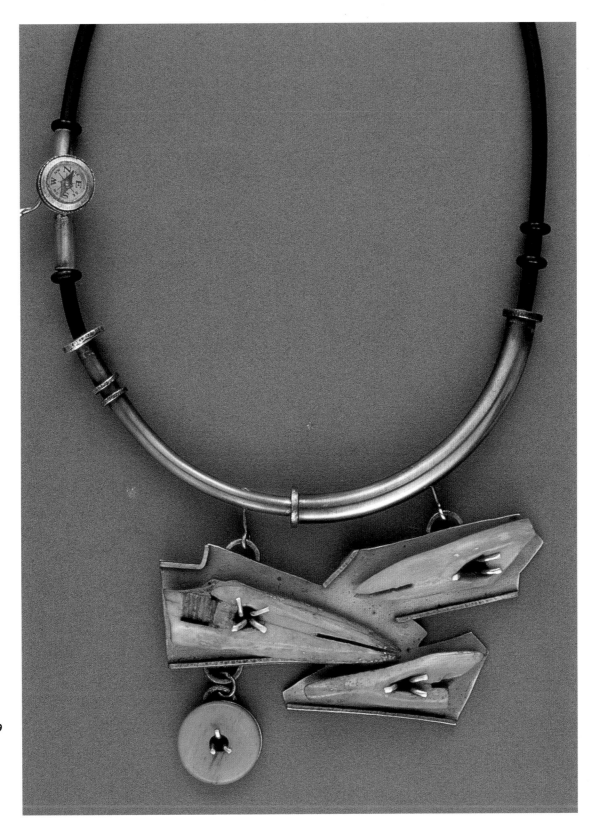

28. *Kimono*, 1999
Silver, African ivory, beach pebble, rubber cord (cat. 57)

29. *Seldovia*, 1999
Copper, silver, Alaskan harpoon holders, rubber cord (cat. 58)

49

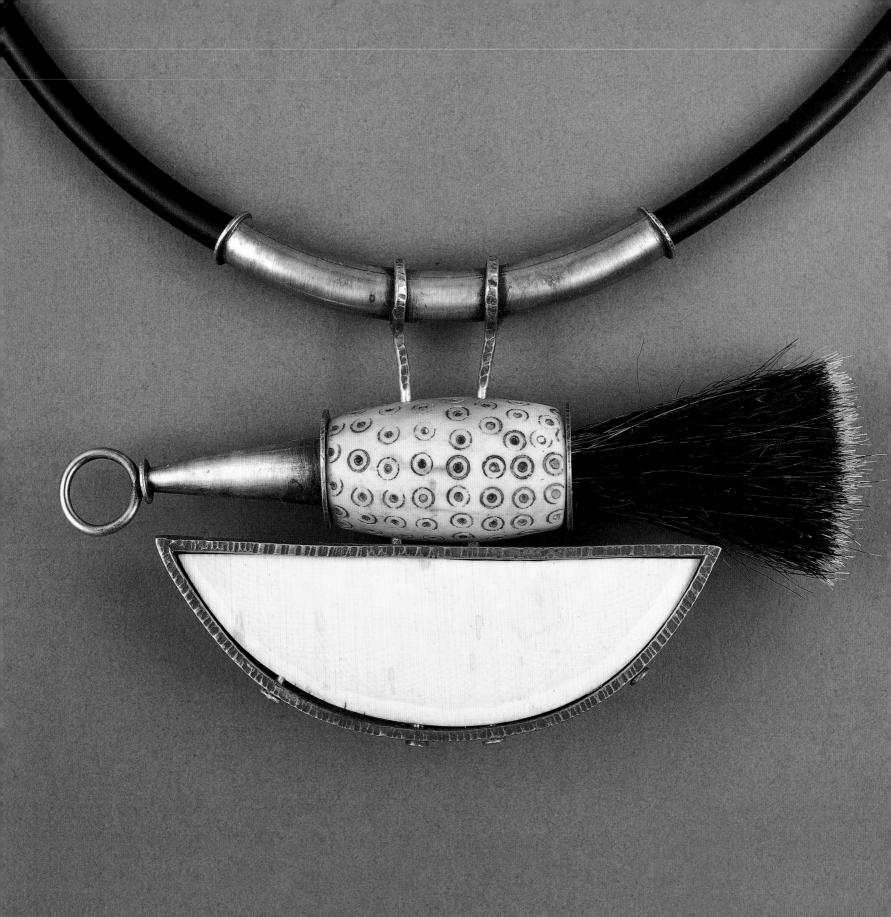

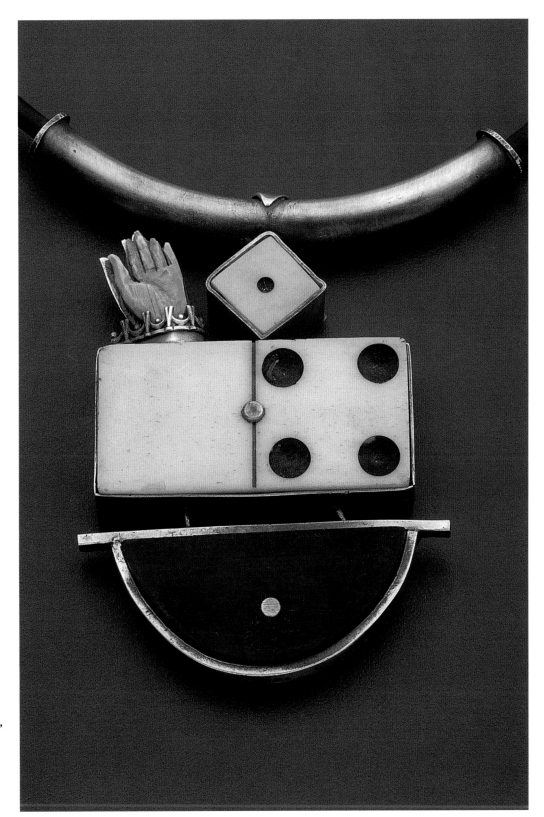

30. *Bavarian Brush*, 1999 Silver, fur hat ornament, Alaskan ivory, Indian bead, rubber cord (cat. 59)

31. *Look I'm a Winner*, 2000 Silver, domino, die, ebony, Indian bone hand, rubber cord (cat. 60)

51

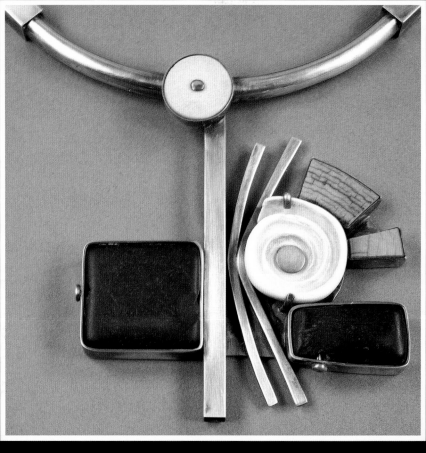

32. *Jet Stream*, 2000 Silver, jet, ivory, shell, bone, rubber cord (cat. 61)

Ramona Solberg, 2001

CHRONOLOGY

1921   Born in Watertown, South Dakota. Lives in Seattle.

Education

1950   Bellas Artes, San Miguel de Allende, Mexico

Universidad de Michoacan, Morelia, Mexico

1951   B.A., Art Education, University of Washington, Seattle

1953–54 Statens Kunst og Handverk Skole, Oslo, Norway

1957   M.F.A., University of Washington, Seattle

1964   University of Arizona, Tucson

Honors

1975   Fellow of the American Craft Council

1987   Washington State Governor's Award

Teaching

1951–56 James Monroe Junior High School, Seattle

1956–67 Associate Professor of Art,

Central Washington State College, Ellensburg

1967–75 Associate Professor of Art, University of Washington, Seattle

1975–83 Professor of Art, University of Washington, Seattle

One-Person Exhibitions

1970   *The Jewelry of Ramona Solberg*, Gima Gallery, Honolulu, Hawaii

1972   Boise State College, Boise, Idaho

Master Crafts: Northwest Award Winners (W. Ron Crosier,
Richard Marquis, Ramona Solberg, Pat McCormick),
Henry Gallery, University of Washington, Seattle (traveling
throughout Washington, Oregon, Idaho, and Montana)

1973   Departure Gallery, Tucson, Arizona

1974   Fred Cole Gallery, Seattle, Washington

1976   Anchorage Museum of History and Art, Anchorage, Alaska

1984   African Art Gallery, Tucson, Arizona

1990   Facere Gallery, Seattle, Washington

2001   *Findings: The Jewelry of Ramona Solberg*, Bank of America
Gallery, Seattle, Washington (traveling retrospective exhibition)

Selected Group Exhibitions

1961   *Northwest Annual Craft Exhibition*, Henry Gallery,
University of Washington, Seattle (award)

1967   *Washington State Governor's Invitational*,
State Capitol Museum, Olympia, Washington

1968   *World Crafts Council Exhibit*, Lima, Peru

1969   *Objects: USA* (Johnson Wax Collection), Smithsonian Institution,
Washington, D.C. (international traveling exhibition)

Pacific Dimensions IV, Crocker Gallery, Sacramento, California

	Crafts Invitational, State Capitol Museum, Olympia, Washington (also 1973, 1999)
1970	Curator of ethnic jewelry exhibition for Whatcom Museum of History and Art, Bellingham, Washington
	World Craft Exhibition, Dublin, Ireland
1971	*Northwest Craftsmen's Exhibition*, Henry Gallery, University of Washington, Seattle (catalogue, also 1973)
	Object Makers, Utah Museum of Fine Arts, University of Utah, Salt Lake City
1972	*Creative Jewelry*, Design Center, Manila, Philippines
1973	*Ramona Solberg and Jack Smith*, Boise State College, Boise, Idaho
	Made With Metal, Eastern Washington State College, Cheney, Washington
	American Craft Council Northwest Regional Exhibition, traveling metal exhibition (Ramona Solberg, curator)
	American Metalsmiths, DeCordova Museum, Lincoln, Massachusetts
	19 American Metalsmiths, Elements Contemporary Crafts, Greenwich, Connecticut
1975	*Mainland Craftsmen*, Honolulu Art Academy, Honolulu, Hawaii
1976	*Ramona Solberg and Ron Ho*, Northwest Craft Gallery, Seattle, Washington
1979	*Fired Arts*, Bellevue Art Museum, Bellevue, Washington
1981	Faber Gallery, New York, New York
1982	*Good as Gold*, Smithsonian Institution Traveling Exhibit
	Ramona Solberg and Paul Soldner, Elements Contemporary Crafts, Greenwich, Connecticut
	Scan Design, Seattle Center, Seattle, Washington
	Contemporary Jewelry, Eastern Washington University, Cheney, Washington
1983	*Ramona Solberg and Laurie Hall*, Elements Gallery, New York, New York

1985	*Lost and Found: Ramona Solberg, Kiff Slemmons, Ron Ho, and Laurie Hall*, Traver-Sutton Gallery, Seattle, Washington
	Elaine Potter Gallery, San Francisco, California
1986	Cheney Cowles Museum, Spokane, Washington
1987	*Ubiquitous Bead*, Bellevue Art Museum, Bellevue, Washington (Ramona Solberg, curator and exhibitor)
1988	*Professors' Choice*, Lang Gallery, Scripps College, Claremont, California
1989	*Washington Crafts, Then and Now*, Tacoma Art Museum, Tacoma, Washington
1990	*Take Five*, Facere Jewelry Art, Seattle, Washington
1991	*Masterworks: Pacific Northwest Arts and Crafts Now*, Bellevue Art Museum, Bellevue, Washington
	Sylvia Ullman American Crafts Gallery, Cleveland, Ohio (also 1993)
	Artists at Work—Twenty-five Northwest Glassmakers, Ceramists, and Jewelers, Cheney Cowles Museum, Spokane, Washington
	Holiday Collectibles, Sylvia Ullman American Crafts Gallery, Cleveland, Ohio
1992	*Of Magic, Power, and Memory: Contemporary International Jewelry*, Bellevue Art Museum, Bellevue, Washington
1993	*The Bead Show*, Hand and Spirit Gallery, Scottsdale, Arizona
	Works Gallery, Philadelphia, Pennsylvania
	Living Treasures, Sybaris Gallery, Royal Oak, Michigan
	Lifetime Achievements: The American Craft Council College of Fellows in Metal, National Ornamental Metal Museum, Memphis, Tennessee
	Documents Northwest: Six Jewelers, Seattle Art Museum, Seattle, Washington
	Northwest Echo: Three of Six (Flora Book, Mary Lee Hu, Ramona Solberg), Facere Jewelry Art, Seattle, Washington
	Screams With Laughter: Storytelling in Northwest Craft, Bumbershoot Arts Festival, Seattle Center, Seattle, Washington

1994	*Two Friends: Ron Ho and Ramona Solberg*,
	Facere Jewelry Art, Seattle, Washington
	One of a Kind, Mobilia, Cambridge, Massachusetts
1995	*Women Across the Arts*, Washington State Convention
	and Trade Center, Seattle
	Art Jewelry, An Historical View, Facere Jewelry Art,
	Seattle, Washington
1996	*25 at 25*, Society for Contemporary Crafts,
	Pittsburgh, Pennsylvania
	Talking Beads, Facere Jewelry Art, Seattle, Washington
1997	*The Bead Show*, Facere Jewelry Art, Seattle, Washington
1998	*Torch Songs: Fifty Years of Northwest Jewelry*,
	Tacoma Art Museum, Tacoma, Washington
	Brooching It Diplomatically: A Tribute to Madeline K. Albright
	(international traveling exhibition organized by
	Helen W. Drutt English)
	Ubiquitous Bead II, Bellevue Art Museum, Bellevue,
	Washington (Ramona Solberg, curator and exhibitor)
2000	*Ramona Solberg, Robert Ebendorf, and Boris Bally—*
	Past Form-Present Tense: Found Object Jewelry,
	Sybaris Gallery, Royal Oak, Michigan
	Fun and Games, OXOXO Gallery, Baltimore, Maryland
	Under the Influence: Northwest Jewelry and Ethnographic Objects,
	Tacoma Art Museum, Tacoma, Washington

Films

1962	*Jewelry: Beads* (with Frank Bach), Neubacher Films,
	Los Angeles, California
1969	*Papier Mâché; Macrame; Simple Jewelry from Found Materials;*
	Simple Jewelry from Everyday Materials (film strips),
	Jack Stoops Production, Bailey Film Associates, Hollywood,
	California
1970	*Folk Art in Latin America* (with Jack Stoops and Hazel Koenig),
	Bailey Film Associates, Hollywood, California

Public Collections

American Craft Museum, New York

Jacksonville Art Museum, Florida

King County Arts Commission, Washington

Renwick Gallery, Smithsonian Institution, Washington, D.C.

Tacoma Art Museum, Washington

SELECTED BIBLIOGRAPHY

Allan, Lois. "Ramona Solberg," in *Northwest Originals: Washington Women and Their Art*. Portland, Oregon: MatriMedia, 1990.

Benesh, Carolyn L. E. "I'm sort of the Henry Ford of jewelry." *Ornament*, Autumn 1989.

Biskeborn, Susan. *Artists at Work*. Seattle and Anchorage: Northwest Books, 1990.

Cetlin, Cindy. "Art, Artifact and the Jewelry of Ramona Solberg." *Metalsmith*, Summer 1985.

de Cerval, Marguerite, ed. *Dictionnaire International du Bijou*. Paris: Editions du Regard, 1998.

DiPasquale, Dominic. *Jewelry Making: An Illustrated Guide to Technique*. Englewood Cliffs, NJ: Prentice-Hall, 1975.

English, Helen W. Drutt, and Peter Dormer. *Jewelry of Our Time*. New York: Rizzoli, 1995.

Halper, Vicki. *Documents Northwest: Six Jewelers*. Seattle: Seattle Art Museum, 1993.

Herman, Lloyd. *Good as Gold: Alternative Materials in American Jewelry*. Washington, D.C.: Smithsonian Institution Traveling Exhibition Service, 1981.

Johns, Barbara, ed. *Jet Dreams: Art of the Fifties in the Northwest*. Tacoma, WA: Tacoma Art Museum, 1995.

Kangas, Matthew. "Ron Ho and Ramona Solberg: Jewelry as Art and Adornment." *Seattle Times*, November 7, 1994.
——. "The Age of Solberg," *Metalsmith*, Winter 1995.
——. "Ellensburg Funky," *Metalsmith*, Fall 1995.
——. "Pacific Northwest Crafts in the 1950s," in Barbara Johns, ed., *Jet Dreams: Art of the Fifties in the Northwest*.

Kirkham, Pat, ed. *Women Designers in the USA 1900–2000: Diversity and Difference* (New Haven: Yale University Press, 2001).

Lewin, Susan Grant. *One of a Kind: American Art Jewelry Today*. New York: Harry N. Abrams, 1994.

Liu, Robert K. *Collectible Beads, A Universal Aesthetic*. Vista, CA: Ornament, 1995.

McEldowney, Mia. *Under the Influence: Northwest Jewelry and Ethnographic Objects*. Tacoma, WA: Tacoma Art Museum, 2000

Mitchell, Ben. *The Jewelry of Ken Cory: Play Disguised*. Tacoma, WA: Tacoma Art Museum, 1997.

Moseley, Spencer. "The Necklaces of Ramona Solberg," *Craft Horizons*, June 1973.

Noll, Cece. *Torch Songs: Fifty Years of Northwest Jewelry*. Tacoma, WA: Tacoma Art Museum, 1998.

Nordness, Lee. *Objects: USA*. New York: Viking, 1970.

Phinney, Susan. "Objects of Her Affection." *Seattle Post-Intelligencer*, November 6, 1997.

Silberman, Robert. "Video: Ramona Solberg: Jeweler, Teacher, Traveler." *American Craft*, October/November 2000.

Solberg, Ramona. "Variations in Decorative Materials as Combined with Metal in Jewelry." Master of Fine Arts Thesis, University of Washington, Seattle, 1957.
——. *Inventive Jewelry-Making*. New York: Van Nostrand Reinhold, 1972.
——. "On the Other Hand." *By Hand*, 1978.

S.S.J.K., "Exhibition Reviews, 'Lost and Found.'" *Ornament*, Autumn 1986.

Thompson, Sharon E. "People Pieces." *Lapidary Journal*, November 1997.

Untracht, Oppi. *Jewelry: Concepts and Technology*. New York: Doubleday and Company, 1982.

Washington Crafts, Then and Now, Tacoma Art Museum, 1989.

Willcox, Donald J. *Body Jewelry*, International Perspectives. Chicago: Henry Regnery, 1973.

Film
Ramona Solberg—Jeweler, Teacher, Traveler. Directed by Ann Coppel. Produced by The Living Treasures Committee of Northwest Designer Craftsmen, Seattle, 2000.

CATALOGUE OF THE EXHIBITION

Dimensions are in inches. Length (circumference) of the necklace precedes height and width of the pendant when applicable.

1. Pendant with earplug, 1950 (pl. 1)
Silver, pre-Columbian clay earplug; 2 1/4" h x 2 1/4" w;
Collection of the artist

2. *Mitla* (pendant/brooch), ca. 1951 (pl. 2) Silver, pre-Columbian clay artifact; 3" h x 2 1/4" w;
Collection of the artist

3. Pearl necklace, 1953
Silver and pearls; 17" l;
Collection of Priscilla Chong Jue

4. Brooch and earrings, ca. 1957
Silver and dentalium shells
brooch: 1 7/8" h x 1 3/4" w;
earrings: 1 1/4" h x 3/4" w each;
Collection of Carolyn Price Dyer and M. Clark Dyer

5. Pendant with pebbles, ca. 1957 (pl. 3) Silver, gold leaf, beach pebbles, leather; 28" l, 3" h x 2" w;
Collection of the artist

6. Rectangular pendant, ca. 1957
Silver, brass, ivory, and ebony;
16" l, 3" h x 1 1/2" w;
Collection of the artist

7. Beaded necklace, 1961
Silver, ancient glass beads;
15" l, 1 3/4" h;
Collection of Caryl Roman

8. Brooch, 1961
Silver and enamel; 1 3/4" h x 2 3/4" w;
Collection of Gloria E. Crouse

9. Domino necklace, 1967† (pl. 4)
Silver and dominos; 21" l,
3 5/16" h x 1 7/8" w;
Collection of the Jacksonville Museum of Modern Art, Florida

10. *Shaman's Necklace*, 1968 (pl. 5)
Silver, penny, Brazilian *figa*,
Guatemalan *milagro*, Alaskan
artifacts; 19" l, 4 3/8" h x 4 1/2" w;
Collection of the American Craft Museum, New York. Gift of the Johnson Wax Company, from *Objects: USA*, 1977. Donated to the American Craft Museum by the American Craft Council, 1990

11. *Pay Day*, 1969 Silver, overall button, watch winder, Asian gambling pieces, Mexican *milagro*;
21" l, 3" h x 5" w; Collection of Anne Gould Hauberg

12. Eagle pin, 1970 Silver, enamel peace symbol, cast WAC eagle, and newsprint mat; 5 1/4" h x 4 1/2" w;
Collection of the artist

13. *Eskimo Chain*, ca. 1970 (pl. 6)
Silver and Alaskan ivory artifacts;
23" l; circular pin: 1 1/2" diameter;
Collection of Ruth McLuckie

14. Doodley-Doo necklace, 1972 (pl. 9) Doodley-Doo
(PVC); 18 1/2" l, 5" h;
Collection of Marion Gartler

15. Felt necklace, 1972 Felt, thread, mirrors, beads; 31" l, 3 1/4" h;
Collection of the artist

16. Plastic pouch necklace, 1972 (pl. 8) Plastic, chicken leg bands, found objects, yarn;
23" l, 5" h x 3 1/2" w;
Collection of the artist

17. Millefiore necklace, ca. 1972 (pl. 7) Electroformed silver and African millefiore beads; 25 1/2" l;
Estate of Jean Jongeward

18. *Coral Branch*, 1972 Cast silver, bronze, and coral; 21 1/2" l, 3" h;
Collection of Eveleth Green

19. *Mali*, 1972 (pl. 10) Silver, ostrich eggshell beads, African ivory;
20" l, 3 1/4" h x 2 1/8" w;
Collection of Marjorie Day

20. *Series 2*, 1972 (pl. 11)
Silver, brass ship and locker tabs, leather; 20" l, 4" h x 2 1/2" w;
Collection of Leslie Campbell

21. Shell necklace, early 1970s* Cast silver, African shell beads; 20 1/2" l;
Collection of Ella Steffens

22. Shell necklace, early 1970s
Cast silver, Niger River shell beads;
22 1/2" l;
Collection of Ron Ho

23. *Tantric*, 1970s
Silver, skull bone beads, leather;
21 1/2" l, 2 3/8" h x 3" w
Estate of Beaudette Smith

24. Silver necklace, 1967, reconfigured 1975 Silver, lapis, coral, and turquoise; 22" l, 7 1/2" h;
Collection of Caryl Roman

25. *Coral Bush*, 1977 Silver and coral; 2 strands: 25" and 28" l;
Collection of Anne Gould Hauberg

26. Domino necklace, 1978* Silver, dominos, underwear buttons, leather cord; 21" l, 3 3/8" h x 2 1/2" w;
Collection of Ella Steffens

27. *Watership Down*, 1978 (pl. 12) Cast silver and compass pendant; 3 1/2" h x 2" w;
Collection of P. Cameron and Bobbie DeVore

28. *South Pacific*, 1979* (pl. 13)
Silver and shell beads; 23" l;
Collection of Ella Steffens

29. *Button Rule*, 1981 (pl. 14)
Silver, found buttons and caliper, leather; 22 1/4" l, 4" h x 3 3/4" w;
Collection of Marion Gartler

30. **Game piece pendant, ca. 1981** Cast silver, ebony game piece, Japanese bead, ostrich eggshell; 20" l, 4" h x 2 1/4" w; Collection of Kim Travenick

31. *Ampersand*, **1982 (pl. 15)** Silver, found ivory ampersand, ruler, leather; 22 1/2" l, 3 1/4" h x 3 1/2" w; Collection of Sue Hovis

32. *Mudra*, **1983** Cast silver and bronze, copper, Indian ivory hand, African beads; 31 1/2" l; King County Arts Commission Collection

33. *Camel Cage*, **1983** Silver, camel bone beads; 25" l; Tacoma Art Museum, Gift of Flora Book

34. **African bottle bead necklace, 1983 (pl. 16)** Cast silver and glass beads; 20 1/4" l; Collection of Ngaire Hixson

35. **Untitled (friendship card necklace), 1983–4** Antique card, beads, mirror, Plexiglas, silver, brass; 23 1/2" l, 3 5/16" h x 5" w; Tacoma Art Museum, Gift of the artist

36. **Coral necklace, early 1980s (pl. 17)** Cast silver and coral beads; 28" l; Collection of Nancy Worden

37. *Chicago Fire*, **1985 (pl. 18)** Silver, dominos, buttons, leather; 21" l, 3 3/8" h x 2 3/4" w; Collection of Charyl Kay Sedlik

38. *Lucky 7*, **1986 (pl. 19)** Silver, Czech plastic disks, ebony game pieces; 22 1/2" l, 2 5/8" h x 2 1/2" w; Collection of Nora Smids

39. *Conus*, **1988** Silver, bronze, African conus shells, leather; 22" l, 4 1/2" h x 5" w; Collection of Helen Houston

40. *Chinese Gambler*, **1989** Silver, game pieces, ivory hand, Chinese coin, leather; 22" l, 3" h x 5" w; Collection of Alida Latham

41. *Naga*, **1989*** Silver and Burmese amber beads; 25" l; Private collection

42. *Lombok*, **late 1980s** Silver, Indonesian lime container; 25" l, 4" h x 4" w; Collection of Beverly Martin

43. *There's a Rabbit in my Garden*, **1990** Cast and forged silver, compass, Asian artifacts, Japanese cord; 20 1/2" l, 3 1/8" h x 3 3/4" w; Collection of LaMar Harrington

44. **Amber necklace, ca. 1990** Cast bronze, silver, amber beads; 21" l; Collection of Erica Williams

45. *Pinto Pony*, **ca. 1990** Silver, bronze, shell, beads; 25 3/4" l, 2 3/4" h; Collection of Natalie Albers

46. *Labrets*, **1991** (pl. 20)** Silver, pebbles, African and Eskimo labrets, leather; 20 1/2" l, 2 1/2" h x 3 3/4" w; Collection of Sylvia Ullman

47. *Lucky 13*, **ca. 1992 (pl. 21)** Silver, domino, dice, cord; 24 1/4" l, 3 1/2" h x 1 1/4" w; Collection of Virginia Washburn

48. *The Game*, **1993** Silver, pebble, bone beads, game piece, leather; pendant: 3 1/8" h x 3" w; Collection of Bill Nelson

49. *Bow Regards*, **1994 (pl. 22)** Silver, violin bow parts, Victorian mother-of-pearl pin, rubber cord; 28" l, 4" h x 4" w; Collection of Mary Pigott

50. **Game piece necklace, 1994** Silver, silver earring, game pieces, leather; 23 5/16" l, 2 7/16" h x 2 1/4" w; Collection of Anita R. Gilmore

51. *Russian Trader*, **early 1990s** Silver, glass trade beads; 26 1/4" l; Private collection

52. *Cracker Jack Choo Choo*, **1995 (pl. 23)** Cast and forged silver, compass, map, button, Lucite, leather; 26" l, 3 3/4" h x 4" w; Collection of Jean Anderson

53. *Time Flies*, **1995 (pl. 24)** Silver, clock face, bone ornament, plastic fly, rubber cord; 25 3/4" l, 3" h x 3 1/8" w; Collection of Susan C. Beech

54. *Indian Bank*, **1995 (pl. 25)** Silver, copper, coins, tin bank, leather cord, electroformed arm; Arm electroformed by Nancy Worden; 29 1/2" l, 5" h x 3" w; Private collection

55. *Mr. McGregor's*, **1996 (pl. 26)** Silver, Chinese ivory rabbit, enameled carrot, millefiore beads; 4" h x 11" w; Collection of Sharon Setzler

56. **Necklace with bee, 1985, reconfigured in 1997 (pl. 27)** Cast silver, Indian ivory, Lucite, bone beads, leather; 30 1/2" l, 4" h x 6" w; Collection of Ella Steffens

57. *Kimono*, **1999 (pl. 28)** Silver, African ivory, beach pebble, rubber cord; 24" l, 2 1/2" h x 3" w; Collection of Julie Spiedel

58. *Seldovia*, **1999 (pl. 29)** Copper, silver, Alaskan harpoon holders, rubber cord; 22" l, 3" h x 5" w; Collection of Alida Latham

59. *Bavarian Brush*, **1999 (pl. 30)** Silver, fur hat ornament, Alaskan ivory, Indian bead, rubber cord; 33" l, 4" h x 6" w; Collection of Daphne Farago

60. *Look I'm a Winner*, **2000*** (pl. 31)** Silver, domino, die, ebony, Indian bone hand, rubber cord; 28 1/2" l, 3 1/4" h x 2 3/4" w; Collection of Elsie Fergusson

61. *Jet Stream*, **2000 (pl. 32)** Silver, jet, ivory, shell, bone, rubber cord; 22 1/2" l, 4" h x 3 3/4" w; Courtesy of Facere Jewelry Art, Seattle

Pieces by Other Artists

62. Laurie Hall
Rule of Thumb, 1985
Cast silver, wood, polymer,
brass ruler; 28" l;
Collection of Ruth Newman

63. Laurie Hall
An Account, 1994 (illustr. p. 15)
Brass; 22" l, 4 1/4" h;
Collection of Mimi Santal

64. Ron Ho
All Fall Down II, 1981 Silver,
ebony, ivory, domino,
buttons; 26" l, 3 3/4" h x 3 1/8" w;
Tacoma Art Museum,
Gift of Ramona Solberg

65. Ron Ho
The Kingfisher and the Tigers,
1990 (illustr. p. 14) Silver, antique
Chinese hair ornament, silk
cording; 26" l, 5 1/4" h x 5" w;
Collection of Virginia Washburn

66. Ruth Penington
Untitled (moonstone necklace),
n.d. (illustr. p. 5) Silver, moon-
stones, agates, opals; 14" l;
Tacoma Art Museum,
Gift of Gene and Liz Brandzel

67. Ruth Penington
Untitled (ermine tail necklace),
1971 Silver and ermine tails; 17" l;
Tacoma Art Museum,
Gift of Anne Gould Hauberg

68. Kiff Slemmons
Hands of the Heroes: Colette, 1987
Silver, garnets, found objects;
3 1/4" h x 2 1/2" w;
Collection of Sandy Grotta

69. Kiff Slemmons
Hands of the Heroes: Ramona,
1991 (illustr. p. 17) Silver, amber,
beads; 3 1/4 h x 2 7/8 w;
Tacoma Art Museum,
Gift of Ramona Solberg

70. Kiff Slemmons
Paisley, 1998 (illustr. p. 17)
22" l, 2 3/4" h;
Collection of Anita Kaplan

71. Don Tompkins
*Commemorative Medal
Series: Hugh Hefner*, ca. 1970
(illustr. p. 9) Silver, wood, found
objects; 3 1/4" h x 4 1/4" w;
Collection of Maryn Tompkins

72. Don Tompkins
*Commemorative Medal Series:
Richard Nixon*, ca. 1970
Silver, gold, Plexiglas, found
objects; 4 3/4" h x 5 1/16" w;
Collection of Maryn Tompkins

73. Nancy Worden
Initiation Necklace, 1977
Silver, copper, rhodonite, plastic,
ribbon; 28" l, 3" h x 3 1/2" w;
Tacoma Art Museum,
Gift of the artist

74. Nancy Worden
Viper's Venom, 1998
(illustr. p. 18) Copper, silver,
python skin, glass taxidermy
eyes, found objects; 24" l, 2" h;
Courtesy of William Traver
Gallery, Seattle

*Exhibited in Seattle and
Charlotte, N.C. only

** Seattle and San Francisco only

***Seattle, Charlotte, and
San Francisco only

† Seattle only

PHOTO CREDITS